20 Years of KDE

Lydia Pintscher (Editor)

20 Years of KDE

Past, Present and Future

The information in this book is distributed on an "As Is" basis, without warranty. While every precaution has been taken in the preparation of this work, neither the authors nor the editor or publishers shall have any liability to any person or entity with respect to any loss or damage caused or alleged to be caused directly or indirectly by the information contained in it.

Copyright © 2016 Sandro Andrade, Sanjiban Bairagya, Pradeepto Bhattacharya, Mirko Boehm, Scarlett Clark, Ben Cooksley, Andreas Cord-Landwehr, Matthias Ettrich, David Faure, Mario Fux, Timothée Giet, Frederik Gladhorn, Martin Gräßlin, Boudhayan Gupta, Dani Gutiérrez Porset, Vishesh Handa, Riccardo Iaconelli, Volker Krause, Sebastian Kügler, Sinny Kumari, Antonio Larrosa, Richard J. Moore, David Narváez, Baltasar Ortega, Kévin Ottens, Thomas Pfeiffer, Nuno Pinheiro, Lydia Pintscher, Aleix Pol i Gonzàlez, Jens Reuterberg, Cornelius Schumacher, Bhushan Shah, Yash Shah, Aracele Torres, Albert Vaca, Sune Vuorela, Franklin Weng, Valorie Zimmerman

This work is licensed under a Creative Commons Attribution-ShareAlike 3.0 License. To view a copy of this license visit: http://creativecommons.org/licenses/by-sa/3.0/legalcode.

ISBN: 978-1-365-35997-2

*for gearheads
all around the world*

Our vision:
A world in which everyone has control over their digital life and enjoys freedom and privacy.

Thank You!

This book would not have been possible without the support of each of the authors and the following people, who helped make it happen:

- Alejandro Daniel Wainzinger Mateu
- Aleix Pol i Gonzàlez
- Celeste Lyn Paul
- Frederik Gladhorn
- Valorie Zimmerman
- Volker Krause
- Will Stephenson

Contents

1 KDE Ceased to Be Software and Has Became a Culture 1
2 Serving the End User – a Brief Reflection on KDE's History 5
3 The Values Within 11
4 Continuity through Change 17
5 Did You Know? 21
6 KDE e.V. - the Backbone of the KDE Community 25
7 KDE and Qt 31
8 German Association Law as Secret Superpower 37
9 Who Does the Work Decides 43
10 Meet the Gearheads 47
11 Deals with the Devil 51
12 Defining a Vision and Mission for KDE 59
13 On Subtle Contributions 65
14 The Importance of Face-To-Face Meetings 69
15 Remote Places Make Magic Possible 73
16 KDE in Taiwan 77

17 Building KDE's Community in India	81
18 A Revolution in Itself	85
19 Think Globally, Act Locally	89
20 A User at the Court of KDE Developers	91
21 Why I Chose KDE, and Why KDE Is Family	95
22 Story of a Contributor	99
23 The Motivation behind Contributing to KDE	103
24 My Journey from Documentation to Continuous Integration	107
25 A Place to Stay Forever	109
26 A Learning Paradise	113
27 The Circle of Four Steps to Become a Good Developer	117
28 How We Make Plasma	121
29 Evolution of Windowing Systems	129
30 Twenty Years of Email	133
31 Krita Animation	141
32 The Transient Nature of Design	143
33 Say Yes	149
34 Future Journeys: Which Path to Take?	155

35	Staying Relevant	157
36	Software, Freedom and Beyond	161
37	A New Generation	165

1 KDE Ceased to Be Software and Has Became a Culture

Aracele Torres

Aracele Torres fell in love with KDE technologies in 2007 and in 2010 decided that she should start to contribute to the community. Since then she has made contributions in many areas, such as translation, promotion, artwork, and community management. She travels through Brazil, giving talks about KDE and organizing activities to promote the community. Additionally she participates in the organization of KDE's Latin-America Summit LaKademy since its first edition. She is a doctoral student in the History of Science and Technology, conducting research on the history of digital technology, free software, the internet and related things.

KDE as a software project was born in 1996 when German programmer Matthias Ettrich realized that Unix-based systems were growing, but their interfaces were not user-friendly enough for the end user. It was only three years after the first GNU/Linux distributions had begun to appear and Matthias noticed the absence of a graphical user interface that offered a complete environment for the end user to perform their daily tasks. He thought that for the people who began to consider GNU/Linux as an alternative to proprietary systems, a beautiful and easy to use graphical environment would help a lot. Thus was born the project "Kool Desktop Environment" or simply "KDE". The name was a pun on the proprietary graphical environment very popular at the time, CDE (Common Desktop Environment) that also ran on Unix systems.

One year after Matthias Ettrich's announcement inviting developers to join the project, the first beta of KDE was released. Nine months later came the first stable release. The dream of Matthias and his community of contributors was becoming reality and occupying an important place in the history of free software. The project was maturing and becoming more complex and more complete. Thanks to the collaboration of people worldwide, KDE had grown from version 1 to 2 in 2000, and then to 3 in 2002. In 2008, after very important changes, the community launched the revolutionary version 4. In 2014, the equally innovative version 5 came out that showed in its visual design, framework, and applications that the community is ready for the future.

During this time, a lot had changed in the KDE Community and its technologies. First came the change of KDE's name and its identity. In 2008, the community began to refer to "KDE" as not just a software project, but as a global community. This identity change was made official in 2009 when the community announced this rebranding. The name "K Desktop Environment" was dropped because it no longer represented what KDE had become. This long name had become obsolete and ambiguous, since it represented a desktop that the community has developed. KDE at that point had become more than just a desktop, evolving into something greater: *KDE was no longer the software created by people, but the people who create software.*

Outside observers of the KDE Community may not have noticed, but this rebranding was a turning point in the history of KDE. Through it, the community makes clear its ability to perceive and keep up with the state of the art of computing. The reign of desktops was over and it made no sense to limit KDE to traditional platforms. Therefore, the decision to use only the name "KDE" intended to communicate to users that the community was attentive to the future. "KDE" would not only be synonymous with a limited set of software components, but be synonymous with the international community that produces free technologies for the end user, whether for desktop or mobile devices or other technologies that are yet to come.

In 2012, this rebranding effort was summarized in a manifesto. The "KDE Manifesto" listed core values advocated by the community and it served as an open call: New projects are now welcome under the

KDE umbrella brand. This led to the creation of the KDE Incubator in 2014. The KDE Incubator serves as an integration point for new free software projects that join the community to have the same benefits as the existing KDE projects. This incubator has become home to a variety of projects, from a wiki dedicated to educational topics to a full-fledged Linux distribution.

KDE continues the same trend it has followed the past 20 years, which is inclusive growth. Its founding principle was based on providing users a better desktop experience. It has expanded that view to also offer the best experience on mobile devices. The future is ripe with possibilities for a new generation of devices: cars, smart TVs, refrigerators, stoves, etc. Can you imagine a smart home or even an entire city using the technologies of the KDE Community?

For almost 10 years I have used the technologies that the KDE Community produces. I remember starting with KDE 3.5 when I still did not even know about the social importance of free software. As a user, as a contributor, and as a historian, when I look back at these 20 years of history, the feeling is the same. The KDE project was born from the interest of a group of people who wanted to make computing, especially free and open computing, accessible to all. The 1990s was a time when the GNU/Linux systems became popular and the internet and the web was becoming more present in people's lives. KDE emerged as an important tool in the popularization of free software. Born with the intent to be an interface between a person and the computer, today KDE is an interface between people. KDE unites and connects people through free computing. KDE has become a community that encourages the growth of people and projects, that seeks innovation, and defends the free sharing of information. KDE has move beyond simply being computer software and has evolved to become a culture.

2 Serving the End User – a Brief Reflection on KDE's History

Matthias Ettrich

Matthias Ettrich is a computer scientist living in Berlin and the initiator of KDE. Since then he has been running different software development teams at Trolltech and Nokia. He co-invented Qt Creator and QML, and co-developed several smart phone platforms which were all terminated by either Nokia or Microsoft shortly before or after launch – Nokia X being the latest one. He currently works as distinguished architect at HERE. Matthias is married with children and recently took up playing jazz trumpet again.

Like any other complex project, KDE was created twice. At first as an idea, and secondly as an implementation of the idea in the real world. Looking back, it was astounding how quickly the idea gained legs – and hands – and started to develop its own life. It obviously showed that the timing was right and that many of us thought alike 20 years ago. My Usenet posting would serve as a catalyst which allowed a growing group of people to connect and get started. Yet, this doesn't explain it all. There is still something magic behind what happened in 1996.

Let me explain what I mean.

First, the concept of a complete and friendly user interface for GNU/Linux, where complete means including almost all relevant applications, was crazily bold. If you had suggested building something like this in a commercial company, you would hardly have made the second preparation gate in the product process. Someone would have given you *the look* and the obvious question: "Are you nuts? Do you have any idea how much effort that is? How many developers you would need, and how much time?"

I wasn't totally naïve back then. Thanks to LyX I knew that my estimation skills for software complexity and required time were overly optimistic. Therefore, I consciously tried to downplay the effort and in hindsight probably the one major thing I got right, provided a thought-out, detailed roadmap proposal leading to a minimum viable product. When eating an elephant, take one bite at a time. My plan looked reasonable enough to make success appear plausible if enough developers joined. And so you did and created KDE.

They say that if you want to make people build ships, don't teach them building ships but teach them longing for the sea. That I didn't have to do. Many of us already had a promotional side and truly wanted to make GNU/Linux accessible to the non-geeky rest. Why? Simply because GNU/Linux was objectively the better system, and there was a strong belief that it should be possible to convert the technical advantages of a UNIX system into real added value for users. "End-users" as we called them back then, to differentiate them from those in the know.

So initially, KDE was about better software for non-technical users, with GNU/Linux at its heart. Therefore, KDE software was not supposed to run on Microsoft Windows, not even as a tactical step. I didn't want any compromises in software quality, but use the alleged power of UNIX to the maximum advantage possible. The idea was not to catch up with Windows, but eventually surpass it.

The plan wasn't crazy, only early. In the end, two commercial companies succeeded with the very same plan in ways which nobody could have imagined 20 years ago: Apple with the Darwin-based Mac OS X, which draws from many open source projects also in higher layers of their software stack. And of course Google, which today dominates the smartphone and tablet space with its Android operation system.

Looking back, KDE has achieved great things also on the technical level. I am sure everyone has their own personal list, but here are my top-three technical achievements: (1) XDND, (2) DCOP/D-Bus, and (3) KHTML/Webkit.

1. XDND is a drag and drop protocol conceived in 1998 by John Lindal, with help from Trolltech, GTK+, and Red Hat. While it wasn't strictly speaking a technical achievement of KDE, the combined critical mass of KDE and GNOME was instrumental in establishing a de-facto standard on the X Window System. It seems unbelievable today, but before KDE there was not even an agreed way to implement such basic visual operations on GNU/Linux. To be honest, before KDE there was such a lack of visual applications that there hardly was any need to drag and drop documents either.

2. DCOP, which later turned into D-Bus, highlighted the importance of IPC for building a complex modern system. The GNOME project saw the same need, but was initially stuck in following a Microsoft-style COM approach using CORBA techniques. Android later went further by adding IPC to the kernel, called Binder, and using higher level constructs in Java for transparent IPC (the intents and content providers).

3. KHTML, which later became Webkit, is probably the most influential code base that came out of the KDE project. It played an important role in the rise of Mac OS X and the iPhone. Where would Safari have been without a competitive HTML engine? And where would Mac OS X and the iPhone have been without the competitive web browser Safari had become?

The one chapter in KDE's history which I do not like to remember is the one about the infamous Trolls vs. Gnomes fights. What can we learn from this? First the obvious standard lesson: the more similarities two communities have, the more intense they fight. I do remember discussions with fellow Trolls where we spoke about the odd sequence of events which brought us here, and how we could have easily ended up on the other side, hacking our fingers off in an attempt to make GTK and GNOME more attractive. In hindsight all of that struggle was completely pointless and didn't serve the free software revolution well.

Talking about revolutions, let's quickly remind us how the French revolution killed the king, and after a period of terror it crowned an emperor. Is this a pattern? The free software revolution broke Microsoft's dominant position in operating system software, fought rigorously against each other, and in the end crowned Apple and Google, who both were very smart in using free and open source software to their own advantages. In all fairness, the analogy is flawed like any other analogy: Microsoft certainly wasn't decapitated, but today is no longer seen as potential threat to software freedom, but simply as one highly successful software company among others – one that actively contributes to free software.

Where are we now on the client side? Users have access to an incredible amount of high quality software today, mostly free of charge, and a lot still available in source code. The horror years of DOS and Windows 3.1 or Windows 95/98 are definitely over. Today every kid or grandmother does things with their smartphones which only hackers could do 20 years ago: email, chat, listening to music, browsing the web; and all with multitasking, and without rebooting the machine several times per day. They also participate in virtual communities, something open source projects pioneered due to the technical skills required to do so. In addition, voice over IP, taking and sharing high quality pictures, and detailed searchable maps of the entire globe are standard use cases today. A standard 9 year old today does more geeky things than a hacker when we started – and doesn't even notice. Try to picture in your head what actually happens when you tell your phone that you would want to walk to the next bakery, and the phone guides you there. Such a simple use case will utilize voice recognition, satellite positioning, a massive graph of places trained by zillions of search requests, and a location graph knowing exactly how to get you there, and of course mobile connectivity as most of the interesting computations are not done on the actual device but inside services operated in big data centers. Isn't that mind boggling? Isn't it amazing how much technical complexity can be hidden behind user interfaces every child can operate at ease?

But also the developers are in a very different position today. There is a plethora of great development tools available from compilers to middleware to IDEs and a significant portion of these run cross platform on Windows, Mac OS, and GNU/Linux.

GNU/Linux is an established platform today, not only in data centers, but also on developers' desktops. And KDE continues to play a big role in enabling this. It plays an even bigger role in demonstrating that the allegedly naïve dream of an entirely free and purely community-driven, open stack is indeed possible. And best of all: No animals were harmed and no investor money was burned in achieving this. That's no small thing to be proud of.

Congratulations KDE, on your first 20 years. I will still be around and curious to learn about the next 20 years.

3 The Values Within

Antonio Larrosa

Antonio Larrosa is a mathematician from Málaga (Spain) who has always worked as a software developer. He joined KDE in 1997. He is the author of the first versions of kmid, kpager and others, maintained parts of kdelibs and fixed bugs in nearly all applications when KDE still used CVS. He organized Akademy 2005 and Akademy-es 2014 in the University of Málaga and gave nearly a hundred talks about KDE for users and developers all around Spain from 1998 to 2005. Currently he works in the SLE Desktop Team at SUSE. He was recently elected president of KDE España.

When someone looks at KDE there are many things that can be seen depending on the point of view and the experience of the observer. One can look at KDE and see an intuitive desktop environment and many applications tightly integrated that allow anyone to use the full power of his/her computer in an easy way. In that sense, someone can use KDE for years and only see - and benefit from - the software developed by its developers. From another point of view, if a developer looks at KDE, he or she might see not only the applications but the framework that KDE provides. With KDE Frameworks a developer can quickly write applications that use the full potential of the desktop and integrate with other applications by maintaining a homogeneous look and feel across the desktop.

But KDE is much more than that. It's a community of people doing Free Software for real users. Let's analyze what that sentence means.

A community...

It's a community because there is a link that bonds us together. There is a purpose in what we do: to create software that liberates people when using computers[1]. There is a strong feeling of community in KDE. There are artists, designers, programmers, translators, users, writers and other contributors from all around the world. Literally, from all continents (OK, maybe except Antarctica). Thousands of people organized to create free software in a common direction.

Now I should point out that if you plan to contribute to KDE, my words might be misunderstood so I want to make clear that you shouldn't let that strong feeling of community discourage you. New contributors are welcomed and indeed will feel welcomed and part of the community quite quickly. Contributing to KDE is not only good for KDE, it can help you get in touch with many really good developers, artists, translators, etc. and by getting you real life experience, it will help you build a better resume.

... of people ...

I guess there is no need to state that, even if sometimes it looks like there are, there are no robots and no aliens collaborating at KDE. They are just people like you and me who at some point in their life decided to invest part of their time (sometimes work time, sometimes free time) in making the world a bit better through Free Software. During these 20 years of KDE's existence, I've met computer scientists who collaborated with KDE, but also all kind of engineers, designers, linguists, musicians, mathematicians, physicians, teachers, retired persons and even high school students working at KDE. I remember an anecdote with respect to that from many years ago at an Akademy meeting with a developer still in high school who needed to use vectors in a game he was developing but he hadn't studied

---

[1] Although there are projects to expand this to tablets and mobile phones too.

them in class yet. As a mathematician I offered to teach him what he needed for his game and he learned some math quite ahead of other people his age.

Since KDE contributors come from very different countries with different cultural backgrounds and customs, there is a Code of Conduct that offers guidance to ensure KDE participants can cooperate effectively in a positive and inspiring atmosphere.

... doing Free Software ...

Everything developed in KDE is Free Software. It's stated as such in the KDE manifesto so it's clear that freedom is in the core of our technology. This has many benefits over non-free software. For example, it's the only way KDE can assure that the software will be available for everyone, for all time.

Freedom is a very valuable right that is usually not perceived as worthy of our attention, until it is lost. And there is a real possibility to lose it. It is currently at risk when we use computer systems that can not be analyzed like some televisions which have a microphone always listening in on your own living room conversations and no one can check exactly what it does with everything it "hears". It is at risk too when someone uses computer software whose license (enforced via legal or technical methods) does not allow the owner to share the software with some friend or family member to use in their own computer. And it is also at risk when you have some software that does something close to what you need but you can not modify it (or get someone to modify it) to do exactly what you need.

Those are only three examples, but to solve those problems, among others, Free Software guarantees 4 types of freedom:

- The freedom to run the program for any purpose.

- The freedom to study how the program works, and change it to make it do what you wish.

- The freedom to redistribute and make copies so you can help your neighbor.
- The freedom to improve the program, and release your improvements (and modified versions in general) to the public, so that the whole community benefits.

... for real users.

Users are the most important part of KDE. During these years I have seen people of all types use KDE's software, from infants to nearly 90-year-old elders, from users who were using a computer for the first time to users with many years of experience using all sorts of computers, from 10,000 PCs in elementary schools in Taiwan to 15,000 PCs in the Munich City Council. All of them use KDE's software with usually very positive outcomes.

But sometimes there are problems too. Usually those problems are not much different to problems that would appear in other desktops/operating systems, but with one main difference. If someone finds a problem within KDE's software, the very developers can be reached at bugs.kde.org where any user can file a bug report with the problem he or she found or the improvement he or she thought it would be nice to have in future versions. That way users can participate in the improvement of KDE's software not only for them, but for everyone else. And yes, developers are not offended when someone reports a bug in a nice, educated and useful way. On the contrary, they encourage users to report bugs since they sometimes only appear under some specific circumstances that developers can't always predict or reproduce.

Conclusion

KDE has evolved a lot in 20 years. As you see, the work KDE currently does is important in many different ways: technically (providing an innovative state-of-the art desktop, applications and frameworks), economically (providing free of cost software for everyone to use, thus giving access to developing countries to the same technology the rest of the world uses) and philosophically (providing software that help us maintain our freedom and rights). If you also think this work is important, don't hesitate to join us and help us make the world a bit better, at kde.org.

4 Continuity through Change

Richard J. Moore

Richard Moore joined KDE around 1997, first contributing a little widget that displayed an LED. Over time that expanded to cover areas such as scripting engines, task bars, and networking. He is currently the maintainer of the Qt Network module and CTO at Westpoint Ltd, an internet security company.

When I first started working on KDE it consisted of a window manager (kwm), a file manager (kfm) and a panel to launch things (kpanel) - it has grown a little since then! It was very easy at the time to make a big contribution to the project simply because there was so much that needed doing. My first application was KPaint, quickly followed by KSnapshot which I wrote mainly so I could make screenshots of KPaint. If you had said to me at the time that KSnapshot would continue to be developed and released for 18 years I wouldn't have believed you.

One of the most surprising things about KDE is how much continuity there has been in the code, and the impact of some early decisions. One major feature was Torben Weis' decision to make the network download facilities of kfm available as a library to other applications. This meant that from the start KDE applications had built-in support for editing files on the internet. This might seem obvious now, when 'The Cloud' is such a big buzz-word and everyone has 24/7 internet access but it was pretty revolutionary at the time. Unlike today, most people weren't on the internet at all (and had often never heard of it). Many of the KDE developers had (by the standards of the time) fast internet access when at university, but at home we had modem access at best. It is only in the last few years with the rise of tools such as One Drive, DropBox and OwnCloud that this kind of facility has become available more widely.

An area where KDE has had a global impact is in the browser market. The original KHTMLW widget was replaced by Lars Knoll with the new standards driven KHTML library. This was later picked up by Apple as the basis of WebKit and now forms the basis of the vast majority of web browsers. I think one of the reasons why KHTML was such a success was due to the way KDE is developed. The use of the LGPL license was obviously a factor, but other rendering engines existed with open licenses. Unlike many other projects, KDE has always had a highly distributed developer base which meant that it was always seen as important to keep APIs clean and understandable, and to make it easy for people to work on the code. The emphasis on clean APIs and clear implementations meant that KHTML was a lot easier to work with than its competitors.

The distributed nature of KDE's development had other benefits too. The first KDE conference organised by Kalle Dalheimer in September 1997 brought together people from all over Europe - it was a very exciting and productive weekend. As well as being a fantastic opportunity to build a community, the amount of code that got written (and rewritten) during the conference was astounding. The KDE internationalisation framework was completed during the meeting, and by the end of the weekend we had the whole desktop working in German ready for the press conference! The meeting also had other highlights such as the first demo of KOffice (written of course by Torben) including the ability to embed different types of document - this would eventually become KParts.

If you look at the modern KDE desktop, there is no doubting that it has evolved from those early days. The level of quality now is unbelievable compared to the early releases. This applies both to the code itself via massive improvements in the testing infrastructure, and much more visibly to the design of the interface itself. A modern KDE desktop is a thing of beauty - the older KDE releases were functional but sadly as engineers we had a big blind spot for graphic design.

KDE as a project has evolved too - most notably it has grown in both numbers and become even more diverse. The growth of a strong

KDE community in India to the point where it is now hosting its own KDE conferences is particularly noteworthy. KDE has started taking a more active role in the wider Free Software and Free Culture community for example as an associate organisation of FSFE and through collaboration with groups such as Wikimedia. The continued evolution of the project and community has helped ensure KDE remains relevant despite the ever changing environment it inhabits.

One thing has been constant though throughout my time working with KDE and that has been the people. While the individuals working on the project change over time, the attitude remains the same. The people are intelligent, curious and eager to experiment. I look forward to seeing what they come up with - I'm sure it will be awesome.

5 Did You Know?

David Faure

David Faure joined KDE in 1998, initially for a dialog box for a 'talk' daemon, then contributing to many different parts of the software: file manager, web browser, office suite, email client, core technologies, Qt, and anything else where a bug prevents him from being productive. He works as a software engineer, consultant and trainer at KDAB.

As one of the members of the community who has been active for the longest time, I sometimes see it as my role to transmit the memories and knowledge of the early days to the more recent generation of KDE contributors.

Did you know, that "KDE" initially stood for "Kool Desktop Environment", but the K quickly lost its meaning, because Kool wasn't so cool after all? One of the very early contributors, Kalle Dalheimer, sometimes joked that it meant the "Kalle Dalheimer Environment", of course :-)

Did you know, that choosing Qt as the base technology was just to get started, with the idea that it was really just the GUI bits, and that it would always be an option to switch to another toolkit at some point? Yeah right :)

Did you know, that the very beginning was a window manager (kwm), a panel (kpanel), and the first library classes where KConfig (whose format was inspired by win.ini) and KApplication, as a place where to instantiate the KConfig class? It took us 16 years to get rid of KApplication again (to give KDE Frameworks 5 a more modular design).

Then comes in my hero: Torben Weis. His creativity was amazing. He was not afraid to start huge projects, with excellent architecture and design skills. He started with the file manager kfm, which became Konqueror and also gave birth to KIO. Then he thought "how about I start an office suite?". This is where I came in, to take over maintainership of kfm while he would go and start KOffice (known today as Calligra). He was also a very fast coder, so people assumed he had clones of himself helping him. An old joke in the community is "Torben broke the cloning machine", which explains why we weren't able to benefit from the same trick ourselves. He unfortunately left the project long ago (my interpretation is that he was more into initial designs than long-term maintenance), but his influence on what KDE is today is still very important, and not just because 'kioclient5' shows file:/home/weis/data/test.html in an example :-)

What did we use before git? Subversion. And before that? CVS. And before that? Just an FTP server where people would upload their sources! When I joined CVS was already being used. Oh the memories of that archaic version control system...

- Even 'cvs diff file.cpp' requires a connection to the server, not convenient in an era of 56k modems (I couldn't be connected all day at home, only at university).

- You want to rename a file? You need to ask Coolo (which is Stephan Kulow's nickname).

- On the other hand you could check out a single file from a branch, we lost that feature. OK, I wouldn't say I miss it :)

- Talking about branches, how do you call your feature branch where you rework e.g. KIO's architecture? "make_it_cool" was a very often used branch name. There was definitely something about the word "cool" in those days...

You might have heard that we used CORBA at some point in the past (for component embedding using inter-process communication). Did you know that there were no stable releases with it, only KDE 2.0 alphas and betas? One of them was even codenamed Krash. This experiment (with a CORBA implementation called Mico) didn't prove successful (the worst part that I remember was that we ended up duplicating all of the menu and toolbar APIs as remote procedure calls) so we had to find a replacement, see below.

Did you know, that we had developer meetings before they were called Akademy? I recently saw a discussion where someone said "DCOP was invented at Akademy long ago". This is not exactly right. Before Akademy (which is not just a name, it also means a conference with presentations the first days) we had developer meetings (nowadays known as sprints). And indeed DCOP was invented at one of these. The story is that Matthias Ettrich and Preston Brown got drunk and declared that they would write a CORBA replacement in one night. The result is DCOP (later on replaced with D-Bus, for interoperability with other freedesktop projects, but I'm pretty sure that D-Bus took inspiration from DCOP, so it's an evolution).

Did you know that Trysil was a ski station in Norway? More interestingly it was the location for two KDE developer meetings, the first one just after the switch from CORBA to DCOP. The daily cycle at that event was interesting... Summer in northern Norway means that the sun never really goes down. At 4am the sun becomes slightly less visible for half an hour, and when it comes back up again we would then realize, OK, it's time to go to bed. We'd sleep until noon, have a copious breakfast (well, brunch), hack until dinner, then hack again until 4:30am. Unusual but effective - we got lots done. The hungry mosquitoes are another story though...

Torben joked that he was a bit ashamed of the bad design decision to go with CORBA (and out-of-process component embedding in general), so his next project, with in-process components (which became KParts) was initially called Canossa. Did you know that Canossa is a village in Italy? OK but what's the relation? In January 1077 the Holy Roman emperor Henry IV did penance at the castle in Canossa to obtain a pardon from his excommunication by Pope Gregory VII. We quickly switched to the KParts name though :)

The second Trysil meeting, much later (in 2006, before KDE 4.0), is also a source of very good memories. The contributors coming from America had a bit of a jet lag, so George Staikos was sleeping, sitting on his chair, while his code was compiling, then waking up again to keep hacking/testing. And while Celeste was sleeping on the sofa, other people put a "do not disturb" sign on a sticky note on her head. Meanwhile Coolo was drawing German flags on the forehead and cheeks of anyone who wouldn't run fast enough, due to the Euro Football Championship happening at that time.

All of this, and much more, constitutes the history and culture of our community, and I'm happy to have this opportunity to keep passing it along to more recent contributors. The creativity and enthusiasm of the early contributors is still something we can draw inspiration from today.

6 KDE e.V. - the Backbone of the KDE Community

Mirko Boehm

Mirko Boehm became a KDE contributor in 1997, where he worked on libraries and applications. He was elected a board member of KDE e.V. in 1999, and served in all board capacities from treasurer to president until 2006. He is the author of ThreadWeaver, the concurrency scheduler framework in KDE Frameworks 5. Until 2016, he contributed to KDE as a coder, an auditor and member of the financial working group. Mirko Boehm is a director at the Open Invention Network and the CEO of Endocode. He teaches open source economics at the Technical University of Berlin. Mirko lives with his wife and two kids in Berlin.

In 1996, I was a university student who learned programming in C++ using an incredibly expensive Unix work station. GNU/Linux was the obvious path to program on a similar system after school. However, it was the time of FVWM - a graphical user environment that mainly consisted of a rudimentary window manager with little visual charm and no usability. Using GNU/Linux felt like flying a jet plane, it was very powerful to the initiated, as long as a the user knew what all the knobs and buttons did and all the secret tricks to keep it going. When I learned about KDE, a free software project to build a user-friendly and powerful graphical desktop, I was hooked. I started coding on KDE, learned to love C++ and Qt and grew to be a part of the community. My motivation was mainly to contribute code. There where about two dozen KDE developers at the time, and the community grew quickly. In 1998 I went to LinuxTag in Kaiserslautern. I met many of the other contributors for the first time there. We camped in Kaiserslautern university lecture halls, in sleeping bags on the floor. We talked about visual features and interaction paradigms, performance, communication protocols and software freedom. When I was asked if I wanted to be a member of KDE e.V., I was a bit surprised. Why would a free software community need a registered organization to represent itself?

KDE e.V. is a charitable organization that represents KDE in legal and financial matters. As a legal entity, it is able to accept donations on behalf on the community, and to own the trademarks on the KDE name and logo. I was convinced and I joined. The "e.V." in KDE e.V. stands for "eingetragener Verein", or registered association, in German. This concept exists in Germany in this form since the year 1900. Essentially, it is modeled after a shareholder company where each member (shareholder) holds the exact same amount of shares. Choosing this legal structure implies an important trait of the KDE Community - it is driven by individual contributors, and those contributors are considered equals among peers. If the organization owns assets like a trademark, this asset is effectively jointly owned by the members of the organization. The concept of "eingetragener Verein" implements the ideals of volunteer driven free software communities very well, even though it was contrived long before software was a thing.

In 1999 I was elected to the KDE e.V. board of directors. There where two main tasks - to attain charitable status for KDE e.V., and to rewrite the bylaws so that they are supportive of the large free software community KDE evolved into.

Charitable status for KDE e.V. was not yet granted. Being a charitable organization in Germany is not the same as being a not-for-profit. The organization has to pursue a charitable goal. To a casual observer, it seems obvious that facilitating the development of free software contributes to the common good. Not so for the German financial authorities, who fail to find this aim in the finite list of potentially charitable activities, which does include the advancement of marriage and family or of religion. KDE e.V. finally managed to be granted charitable status, if only through twisting its purpose to fit into the predefined schemes. Once that was achieved, KDE e.V.'s formal structure – a charitable organization with the goal to advance free software and that considered all its members as equals – fits the ideals of a volunteer-based free software community like a glove. It seems like the German legislators would be well-advised to add the advancement of free software to the list of blessed charitable activities.

Re-writing the bylaws proved to be a challenge, because it meant to lay the foundations of governance of the KDE Community as it continued to grow and began to show signs of needing formal structure. To represent the community that understands itself as made up of individual volunteers to the product KDE, the rule that only natural persons could be "active" members (members with a vote) in the organization was kept. To protect the self-determined administration of the community, a rule was adopted that to become a member, a contributor had to be invited by an existing member and endorsed by two more. Considering that every member became a co-owner of all KDE-related assets, such protection was necessary. Directed at preventing hostile takeovers of the organization (the community was still not very big in numbers), this invite-only rule later contributed to the image of KDE e.V. as an exclusive club. Organizations could become "supporting members" if it was in their interest to advance KDE, however this form of membership did not grant them a vote.

Companies that became a part of the community gained a say indirectly by having employees that worked on KDE invited to be members. This was an intended effect that preserved the focus on the individual contributor while still involving organizations. Underlying that was an implicit understanding that the KDE Community should be innovative and directed by the interests and motivation of the contributors, as opposed to commercial interests regarding, for example, the stability and maintenance of existing products. On one hand, this enabled the KDE Community to drastically innovate over multiple generations of its desktop. On the other hand, the rule shut out commercial contributions into the stability and maintenance of existing product versions. As a result, KDE became a beautifully designed and technologically very advanced desktop that sometimes crashed. The focus on individual contributions is based on the idea that self-identification, choosing what to work on based on individual skills and motivations, is the best approach for a software community to stay ahead of the curve. It has served KDE well and became the yardstick for community management when free software finally became mainstream in about 2010.

Similarly important to what an organization is supposed to do is what it is *not* supposed to do. KDE e.V. is not supposed to steer or influence the technical direction of the development of KDE. Its purpose is to be a support organization for the community. In a community that primarily produces software, it is however hard for anyone who participates not to influence technical direction. In the case of KDE e.V., it organizes the annual KDE conference, and finances sprints and other activities. The choice of which development sprints to sponsor or where to be present at a conference does put the spotlight on specific technologies and may influence technical direction.

An important goal of the new bylaws was to account for the regular fluctuation of contributors and to retain the experience of those who for personal or other reasons stopped contributing. The new bylaws introduced the concept of "extraordinary members", individuals that are still members of the organization, but waived their voting rights. It is a way of appreciating their past contributions and offering the opportunity to be part of debates and conversations, while concentrating voting rights in the hands of those that are actively participating.

These "design principles" served KDE e.V. well. It grew to 150 members and more, and was able to regularly collect enough donations to open a permanent office and hire an administrator. It regularly hosts the annual Akademy conferences and runs the hardware and software of the KDE Community. It holds trademarks and represented the community in legal matters. It has become an example for how a free software community can handle its affairs in a self-determined way. Today, KDE e.V. is a large organization with multiple working groups and stable, established processes.

Minor modifications aside, the current setup of KDE e.V. is more or less unchanged since 2003. Over time, some areas have surfaced where reform may be necessary, or is already underway. Many of the discussions between the members have been conducted on the KDE e.V. membership mailing list, which is not open to the public or all contributors. Having such a private list was deemed necessary, but it excluded some contributors from taking part in these discussions. After heated debates at Akademy 2012, a public community mailing list has been created. The norm is now that all debates should be held there unless they require discretion. By preferring lazy consensus and prolonged debate, controversial decisions are hard to make, leading to a practice of bike-shedding. Even though an online voting mechanism has been implemented, it was rarely ever used to ensure that debates could be concluded eventually, and with a productive outcome. This gave vocal minorities or even individuals a de-facto veto and inhibited the implementation of majority opinions. A decision making culture based on consensus works wonderfully well for small groups, but stifles large organizations. Since KDE e.V. does not provide technical leadership to the community, the board and the organization are limited in what they can achieve or in providing direction. A balance needs to be found between maintaining the freedom of the community to innovate, and the ability to coordinate activities within a large group. And finally, there is a lag between changes in the composition of the overall community and the time those are reflected in the membership structure. This provides some stability, but also disconnects the KDE e.V. membership from the larger KDE Community. It is paramount for KDE e.V. to perform well that its membership overlaps as much as possible with the active core contributors of the community.

Most important of all, KDE has changed from being a project that is all about software to a community that is all about people. The KDE Community now invites other projects to come under its umbrella. This marks an important cultural and technological shift, and raises new questions. Should the new sub-projects be represented in KDE e.V., and how? Since the community still consists mainly of volunteers, the design principles of the KDE e.V. bylaws still apply. The basic principles are sound. However, KDE e.V. needs to evolve its processes and rules at the same pace as the community changes and re-invents itself. It will also need to review if the ideals embedded into the current organizational setup still represent why contributors participate in the community.

I am glad that I was offered to opportunity to join KDE e.V. in 1998 and later had the opportunity to serve on the board. After 20 years, KDE e.V. is the backbone of the KDE Community, it provides structure process and continuity. With a bit of maintenance, careful adjustments and by putting the community and its ideals at the center, I am sure the next 20 years can be just as successful.

7 KDE and Qt

Frederik Gladhorn

Frederik Gladhorn started his KDE journey with a small fix to KVocTrain (which he renamed to Parley shortly after) while in Spain in 2005. When he finds some KDE time nowadays, he improves accessibility in Plasma and other KDE software since he values diversity and inclusiveness. Since 2010 he lives in Oslo, Norway to work on Qt for The Qt Company. Recently he worked on the continuous integration infrastructure for Qt. right now his focus is on improving input handling in Qt Quick. That is when he is not marveling at contemporary art, board gaming or outside, surfing, skiing, climbing or doing acrobatics.

Qt is a framework that makes it easy to create applications, especially graphical user interfaces. It is used as the basis for most of the KDE applications and Plasma desktop. Qt provides a wealth of libraries and makes programmers' lives easier. Over time new technologies in Qt were first adapted by KDE and KDE pushed many parts of Qt forward. KDE and Qt always had a strong connection and influenced each other over the years. In this essay I'd like to look back at a bit of shared history.

In 1997 Trolltech started receiving weird bug reports from a certain Matthias Ettrich in Germany. The first Trolltech employee, Arnt, started to get exasperated and said something along the lines of: "These bugs would only matter if you were writing your own window manager". Trolltech at that time consisted of four people, sitting in an otherwise empty building, listening to loud techno and metal music. When they realized, what he was trying to do, there was a hint of doubt, since many projects had recently started with similarly ambitious goals, usually leading nowhere but a small website looking for people to implement the project. Luckily KDE started with a more "show me the code" approach and became a real product not so long after. And it would not take very much longer, before all of Trolltech was running KDE as their desktop of choice.

Trolltech as a company had to keep a strong hold on Qt; it was their product and business after all. But over time KDE influenced the history of Qt in many ways. By the time KDE got started – this was approximately the stone age of free software – Qt was available, under the Qt public license. The QPL was considered not to be compatible with the GPL, but thanks to primarily KDE's interest and dependency on Qt, the license was eventually changed to GPL.

All of this enabled great projects and great cooperation. Did you know that KDE and Trolltech hackers got together in 1998, after Netscape Navigator (yes, that's the browser your parents used which turned into Firefox) got open sourced? They ported the browser to use Qt for the UI, with seven people in an amazing sprint of five days, creating "QtScape" as a proof of concept.

On the people front, over time many a KDE developer started to work on Qt. Yours truly is an example of that, but also Lars Knoll who now holds the CTO position of The Qt Company, but also is the chief maintainer of the Qt Project. Wait, what is a chief maintainer? And the Qt Project, what's that? Let's take a step back; reciting a bit of history is due here.

In June 2008 Nokia acquired Trolltech, leading to a series of changes. All of this time, things could have gone terribly wrong for KDE – after all there is no certainty for anything when big businesses are involved after all. Or is there? Long before the acquisition, a plan was devised to make sure, Qt would be available to KDE, no matter what the future holds. The KDE Free Qt Foundation was conceived as a "poison pill", should any company, current rights owner or future, try to take the freedoms away from Qt. In case of no free and open source release for twelve months, KDE would get the rights to the source code under a permissive license. Long cooperation between individuals inside the commercial Qt business and the KDE Community and the foundation lead to trust and respect from both sides. Over time KDE (represented by the non profit organization KDE e.V.) and the Qt rights holders have worked to refine and improve the terms regulating the foundation together.

Nokia changed things, aiming for as wide distribution of Qt as possible, on desktop and for their phones. The license was changed from GPL to the more permissive LGPL. For the free software world, Qt became a better project in many ways: a proper public bug tracker became finally available. For the first time a system to allow external contributions was put in place: with the help of Gitorious (now defunct) changes to improve Qt could be accepted. For me this is the time of big adventure, moving from Germany to Norway to find out why it wasn't very smooth getting changes accepted into Qt. From the outside it looked deceivingly simple: push the desired change to Gitorious, wait for someone to click the magic button and all was good. The process had some minor and a few major flaws. At first each contribution was checked by a rather large legal department. Assuming it got a green flag, eventually there was no button to click, but a lot of work to do. Running a few scripts, reviewing the change, testing it and then taking full responsibility for it was roughly the process. The amount of work to get anything contributed was often not worth the trouble, which is of course not a sustainable process. The fix for this brings us to another historical development under the reign of Nokia – the Open Governance project for Qt. One thing which was pretty clear was that having two work flows, one for "internal" people and one for contributors on the "outside" was not going to cut it. The open source Qt Project was born to be steered by the community. Making changes to Qt is the same for everyone, reviewing changes is also shared by the entire community. Lead by Thiago Macieira, the development process of Qt was re-shaped and strongly inspired by KDE's. For example the very flat hierarchy of letting any contributor access all repositories works well. The process is merit based, and just like in KDE, where people with more experience often have greater influence and respect get to weigh in on decisions, at the same time sound technical arguments will be listened to, no matter who voices them. Qt started to have a layered system, where it's easy for anyone to contribute changes. Those more involved in the project eventually become approvers, having the right to accept other's changes. Here Qt diverges a little from KDE: each change has to be reviewed. I'm happy to see that in KDE reviews have become the norm in many areas as well. For each area in both KDE and Qt, there are designated maintainers. Many parts of Qt have their maintainer inside The Qt Company, but also quite some are maintained by KDE contributors, holding these important positions, influencing the direction of Qt strongly. To get back to the earlier thread, you guessed, it, at the top of the maintainers for Qt is Lars Knoll, another old time KDE contributor and now maintainer responsible for all of Qt.

Another great story is the Android port of Qt, which was started by BogDan Vatra. Nokia did not want to host the work for Android, but KDE stepped up and hosted the port. Now that Qt is independent again, the port found its proper home inside of Qt itself and KDE applications are being ported to Android.

Eventually in 2012 Digia acquired Qt and the focus shifted from Nokia phones to all of Qt's users. This year, The Qt Company was spun out of Digia and we are independent, shaping the future of Qt with all of you. While The Qt Company takes a big role in making sure the testing and releasing infrastructure is in place, a lot of development of Qt comes from other parties, a significant chunk from many KDE contributors, for that, we'd like to say thank you KDE! There are also events such as Akademy which has been co-located with the Qt Contributors' summit for two times by now. I cannot wait to attend this year's QtCon, bringing together even more and greater communities, among them KDE and Qt contributors.

For me personally, KDE and Qt mean a big group of friends, people I see at work, but also when traveling. People I look forward to meeting all around the globe. KDE has lead me to travel to Nigeria and India, certainly the most memorable and impressive trips in my life. I really wouldn't want to miss that, ever. Special thanks to to all the friendly people that hosted me, taught me, shared flats and went on crazy trips with me. I hope I'll continue to have the chance to learn from you all.

Twenty years have passed, but some things never change: we still get weird bug reports from KDE. And all we can say is: "Keep them coming!" Congratulations to being twenty years young, KDE!

8 German Association Law as Secret Superpower

Cornelius Schumacher

Cornelius Schumacher became a contributor to KDE in 1999. He maintained KOrganizer, co-founded Kontact, wrote KConfig XT and a lot of other code. In addition to coding, Cornelius served on KDE e.V.'s board for nine years, five years of them as its president. Cornelius works as an engineering manager at SUSE Linux. He holds a degree in physics from the university of Heidelberg.

When KDE was founded in 1996 it was off to a quick start. It only took days to find a group of core developers, a few weeks to release the first code, and it quickly gained popularity a couple of months after its inception. In 1997 the founders decided to create a non-profit organization incorporated according to German association law in order to support and represent KDE. This decision turned out to be of remarkable foresight.

When people ask if they should found an organization to support their free software project, the usual advice is: "Don't do it". It comes with a lot of work, with headaches of an unusual kind, and requires quite a bit of stamina to follow through. It's worth it, but it's a heavy investment, which only bears fruits if you can sustain it. Nowadays there are a number of organizations which can act as umbrella for free software projects, and many projects actually have gone through the process of creating their own organization. This was different in 1997. KDE was a pioneer.

The Linux-Kongress took place in Würzburg, Germany, in the spring of 1997. It was one of the primary Linux and free software related events at that time. KDE presented its desktop there for one of the first times. This was an overwhelming success. Two members of another desktop project canceled their presentation and left the event after they had seen Matthias Ettrich and Martin Konold show what KDE could already do. Haavard Nord, one of the founders of Trolltech, presented Qt, the toolkit KDE based its software on. He had conversations with the KDE people, which should shape the future of the project. On the way back home to Tübingen the foundation for creating KDE e.V. was laid and Martin then wrote the first version of the articles of association of what would become KDE e.V.

The founding meeting was scheduled for October 1997 in the student apartment of Matthias Ettrich. German law requires seven people to physically be present as initial members to found an association. As KDE already was a distributed international project back then, they had to recruit Matthias' room mates to meet the required number. The initial members voted about the articles and the association was born. Matthias became its first president, and Kalle Dalheimer and Martin its vice presidents. That out of the way, it's said that the group then quickly turned to technical matters again and established a packet radio connection to the neighbor's apartment.

One of the primary reasons for creating KDE e.V. was the need to handle money for developer meetings. The first KDE meeting in Arnsberg in September 1997 already had a budget of a few thousand Euros, and handling this in a private way was getting impractical. With KDE e.V. there was the right mechanism in place to handle that more professionally, and it turned out to be one of the most powerful catalysts for the community. Hundreds of developer meetings followed and dozens of conferences all over the world. Without KDE e.V. as secret superpower behind it this wouldn't have been possible.

The first critical test for KDE e.V. came in 1998. There was a debate about the license of Qt. Some people held the opinion that it wasn't free enough. Trolltech, the owner of Qt, decided to do something about it and entered into an agreement with KDE that would guarantee the availability of Qt under a free license. The KDE Free Qt Foundation was born, founded by Trolltech and KDE e.V.

Matthias and Kalle flew to Oslo to sign the contracts and established a cornerstone of Trolltech's commitment to free software and KDE.

The agreement of the KDE Free Qt Foundation is a defensive agreement, which comes into effect in the case that Qt wouldn't be released under a free software license anymore. While it hopefully never needs to be exercised it gives KDE a seat at the table when Qt licensing is discussed. In 2008 this suddenly became very important when Nokia announced to buy Trolltech including Qt.

Nokia acted as an exemplary free software citizen. They reached out to the KDE e.V. board as one of the first things after the acquisition. Nokia managers came to Frankfurt, where KDE e.V. had established its first office together with Wikimedia Germany, for a remarkable meeting, and KDE e.V.'s board returned the favor by going to Nokia's headquarter in Helsinki to discuss collaboration and strategy. It was a fruitful time with lots of investment in Qt and KDE as well. It turned out that KDE's strategy outlived Nokia's in the end, though.

The meetings, conferences, and the agreement about Qt are only a few examples of how KDE e.V. backed the community in a way which wouldn't have been possible without an organization such as this. KDE always has been a playful bunch of people, who focused on technology. There are countless examples of brilliant technological innovation in KDE's history. But to operate a community on the scale of KDE did require more than that. There were three domains, which were of special significance here: Representation, support, and providing governance.

When a group of volunteers comes together to work on free software, the means of how technical collaboration happens fall into place quite easily. Tools such as git, mailing lists, or IRC provide the distributed infrastructure to develop and discuss code. The philosophy of free software and its development processes provide a solid base for decision making and coordinating work. Two cornerstones of KDE's philosophy always were the common ownership of code, and the mantra that those who do the work decide.

Sometimes it needs more than that. Entering formal agreements needs an entity which can act on behalf of the community. The KDE Free Qt Foundation is an example from the early days of KDE which is still highly relevant. There are more examples, such as holding the registration of the KDE trademark, owning the kde.org domain, being partner in EU research projects, receiving money on behalf of the community, maintaining copyright through the fiduciary license agreement created by the Free Software Foundation Europe, dealing with legal obligations such as taxes, or simply having a central point of contact for people who need an entry point to the community. This is where KDE e.V. represents the community.

Millions of Euros have gone into the community through KDE e.V. over the years. Lots of individuals support KDE by donations. Companies give back by providing financial support. KDE participates in programs where some money goes to the organization for work and support it provides. KDE has been a partner in Google's Summer of Code in all the twelve years of its existence, and KDE e.V. handles the money which goes into supporting the KDE mentors in the program. This money goes back to the community, helping people to attend conferences or developer meetings, providing technical infrastructure, paying for necessary administrative efforts. This is where KDE e.V. supports the community.

Finally KDE e.V. provides governance to the community. This actually comes with a twist, because KDE e.V. does not control or steer the technical development of KDE software. This was one of the conscious decisions when setting up the organization. The open source development process provides culture and practices to take decisions and run development based on the motivation and responsibility of the individual contributors. This is a powerful concept, which doesn't require a central authority to plan and control actions. It can even be harmful to try to exercise central control in that context. So KDE e.V. decided to stay out of this domain.

KDE e.V. does not stay out of the question who ultimately owns KDE, and who manages its assets. The German association law provides a strong and solid base here. It is used by hundreds of thousands of associations in Germany, and it provides a democratic and transparent base of how to run an organization for the public benefit. This makes sure that KDE can't be bought or hijacked. It always will be in the hand of its constituency, the people who put in their time and effort as contributors. So KDE e.V. is the body who is set up to give legitimacy to efforts within the community and to people who act on behalf of it. This is where KDE e.V. provides governance to the community.

Today KDE e.V. is a well oiled machine, which represents, supports, and provides governance to the community. There is an annual general assembly where its members meet to report about work being done, elect the board and other representatives of KDE e.V., and vote about the main decisions taken by the organization. There are regular reports and discussions about ongoing topics, and there is a team taking care of the daily business. This wasn't always a given, though. There was a critical phase in KDE e.V.'s development, where the sustainability of the organization was threatened.

In the early years of the millennium after the tech bubble imploded, there was less money available for technology. Many people changed projects, some people who were paid to work full-time on free software moved on to other endeavors. This also affected KDE. While the development was in full swing driven by enthusiastic volunteers, the organizational side starved. KDE e.V. was in limbo, because too many active members had gone missing.

In 2002 Mirko Boehm, treasurer of KDE e.V at that time, organized a memorable meeting. He invited the members of KDE e.V. and most of the active core contributors of KDE to a general assembly. The goal was reviving the organization, putting an active board in place, and revising the articles of association to deal with members becoming non-active and setting up the foundation for being officially accepted as tax-exempt non-profit organization for the public benefit.

The meeting took place in Hamburg, hosted by the university of the German armed forces. There were meeting rooms, a computer lab, which was quickly hacked to provide the means to compile KDE software, and dormitories for the short times when people needed to keep up with sleep. Rumors say that they were torn down directly after the meeting.

It took two more years to implement all the decisions but with the changes of the articles of association it defined the modern KDE e.V. in the way it still is in place today. A new board was elected bringing in Eva Brucherseifer who would run the organization for the coming five years. The meeting also facilitated a discussion about KDE's values triggered by a document a young ambitious developer from Canada, Aaron Seigo, had written. Aaron couldn't be present at the meeting in Hamburg, but he had a role in the future of KDE e.V., serving as its president from 2007 to 2009.

KDE e.V. went on a growing trajectory over the subsequent years after the meeting. It was able to provide support to the community again, opened an office, employed Claudia Rauch as a business manager in 2008, and dealt with a lot of the work behind the scenes to run the community, to organize its events, such as the memorable Desktop Summits in Gran Canaria and Berlin in 2009 and 2011, hundreds of developer meetings, and many more.

In 2010 it even signed a Hollywood contract. The production of Robert Rodriguez' Machete wanted to include pictures of KDE software in the movie. So KDE e.V. as owner of the trademark and representative of the community jumped in to sign the agreement and allow Robert de Niro and Lindsay Lohan to communicate via KDE's instant messenger.

It might seem surprising, but the solid base of the German association law, the foresight of the founders to create an organization based on this law, and the relentless work of countless people to run this organization did create a secret superpower for the KDE Community. May the community continue to use it wisely. There is a lot of good to be done.

9 Who Does the Work Decides

Vishesh Handa

Vishesh Handa started his KDE contributing days in early 2010 when he tried to understand the semantics behind the Nepomuk project. He eventually started maintaining it, then killed it, and started maintaining most of KDE's search and metadata infrastructure. When he worked on KDE professionally, he also hacked on KDE Frameworks, KRunner, Plasma and various applications.

Open Source products targeting users are a rare thing. Even rarer are the ones not dominated by a business or specific purpose. KDE is one of those projects that satisfies both those criteria and is therefore quite a unique place.

Most user-facing products have a company behind them. This company often controls the entire product, and works on all parts of it - marketing, distribution, evolution, and development. I have purposely put development at the end, because normally the other parts are what drives the development.

In KDE, we have an organization that helps with certain administrative and legal matters - the KDE e.V. However, they intentionally do not steer the development in any significant way. This results in an inversion of the classical model. We call this mode a "meritocracy" and it is one of the core principles of the KDE Community:

> "The person who does the work decides"

This meritocracy results in many interesting consequences. It has resulted in a community where developers have far greater power because they are ultimately the ones who bring the ideas into light. For a developer, this is great. It has built a strong community centered around technical excellence, and we developers have a lot of autonomy. This coupled with the amount senior members try to mentor the newcomers has created a delightful place to learn and improve as a developer. Also because the developers call the shots - they have to take an active role in all other areas and this makes them grow. It is a kind of Elysium that developers love and still get to work on user facing software.

However, this does not lead to a cohesive product that has a direction and really makes an impact. The product development side where we try to understand the needs of a user and rapidly iterate based on the business requirements and the market are lost. It is even incredibly difficult to figure out how we should market our products as developers and other contributors may have conflicting ideas. Our product quite often develops at minimum because of personal itches to scratch or otherwise with the hope that certain developers will lead the product development. Though it is not guaranteed that the others will follow.

It also results in other non appealing jobs often stagnating, especially proper quality assurance and documentation. We cannot just hire people for these fields.

This way of working is not unique to KDE; however, being a user facing product does compound the challenge significantly. Most other significant open source projects are built around solving technical problems. Here the developers are often keenly aware of the problems faced by the other developers, and decisions can often be made solely on technical merit. In KDE we often do not expect our users to be technically qualified.

Even with this developer controlled model, our community has managed to accomplish a lot. Our most recent desktop shell, Plasma 5, has been the result of a lot of collaboration between designers and developers. The existence of the Visual Design Group shows the developers' willingness to work with others. We have contributors spending time in creating promotional material for KDE and others organizing conferences to mentor newcomers.

For me, however, this is one half of the story. The other half is one which is well known - the evolution of KDE's identity and its interesting consequences.

In KDE we started off as a desktop environment and grew because of our role as a Desktop Environment, and now KDE means the community. However for many, including me, it is a mixture of the desktop environment, certain applications and libraries. But this is also now changing with the inclusion of projects such as Wiki2Learn. It is hard to say who KDE is targeting and figuring this out is a difficult process.

If we adopt a stricter approach we risk alienating existing projects and members while loosening the criteria also results in KDE being no different than "Free and Open Source software", but with a bit more user focus.

These two factors - the developer controlled products, and the gradual decline of a core and actionable identity are for me some of the biggest challenges faced by KDE. It is also what makes it an exciting place.

The obvious conclusion to this is - where do we go beyond these initial 20 years?

The libraries and developer tools will most certainly survive. They suit this model where developers control the direction, specially since they directly target the developers. The desktop shell still fulfills a niche. It probably will continue, though it would be hard to say in what form, and with the world moving towards trendier technological stacks, the shell is certainly losing momentum.

The world of applications is quite different to what it was when we started. Content is what seems to matter. The applications that can help the user work with the content across multiple devices and platforms are the ones that gain more traction. KDE applications are starting to move towards other platforms and compete with the rest of the world, but it is a difficult task, and being "open" does not seem to be an important selling point. They will really need to step up and focus on non-development roles.

Overall, it has been a fun ride over the last 20 years. Many people have come and gone, and KDE's popularity has peaked and fallen. I certainly hope the next generation of developers takes KDE further in this completely different world.

10 Meet the Gearheads

Kévin Ottens

Kévin Ottens has more than 12 years of experience working with Qt. He is also a long term contributor of the KDE Community where he focused for a long time on libraries API design and architecture. Graduating in 2007, he has a PhD in artificial intelligence. In 2012, he participated in the creation of the KDE Manifesto. Nowadays he spends time rethinking his job via a strong interest in Software Craftsmanship. Kévin's job at KDAB leads him to contribute to Qt 3D but also includes giving trainings and the responsibility of community liaison with KDE. He lives in Toulouse where he serves as a part time teacher in his former university.

As I am writing these lines, I am 36 years old. I have been a user of KDE products since 1997. It has been 19 years, almost half of my life, almost as long as the community exists. I finally decided to get involved with KDE as a contributor in 2003, almost a third of my life. Also, I intend to stay involved somehow. If everything goes well (for the community and also for me), at one point my life without KDE will be anecdotal compared to my life with it.

Why am I telling you all this you may ask? Well, I just want you, dear readers, to realize that it has been an awfully long time! And now you might just wonder *"Why? Oh Why? Why would someone in his right mind do something like this? Why spend your youth working on something which won't make you rich or famous? Why even contemplate doing that while being older? Don't you have a life?"*

These are a lot of valid questions and I will try to answer them simply with this: *you can't and shouldn't get rid of your family.* That might still sound mysterious, so let's expand on this idea.

How It All Started

For as long as I can remember, I wanted to do something related to computers and later decided that I'd at least try myself at artificial intelligence topics because of William Gibson's Neuromancer. In 1996, I bumped into my first Linux distribution (a Slackware spin) and got hooked on the Free Software culture as a result. It was only a matter of time before I ended up contributing to something.

I had this hunch that I would likely contribute to something I use and so I tried to use mostly Free Software with source code I felt comfortable with. Yes, it means I chose by looking at the code of the software I evaluated, not by its looks or by how many features it stacked (those criteria came only distant second). Needless to say, that quite a lot of the software at the time wasn't really to my liking. In the end, the source code coming from KDE impressed me the most, so I started to use more and more of it, waiting for an opportunity.

Finally, I found a missing feature for my workflow in the desktop of the time and decided to make a plugin for it. Instead of keeping it for me, I decided to contribute it to the world and was greeted by a crazy Canadian who maintained Kicker at the time. My plugin ended up being a part of the next official release.

That was obviously a very encouraging start. Still, the story thus far has been mostly about technical facts and some distant political vision. Nothing which could explain being engaged for long with the same community.

"Happy Families" Meets the Lunatics

I started for technical reasons, but really, I have stayed because of the people. When I first got into KDE, it sometimes acted like a large, funny and chaotic family. It was also quite dysfunctional at times... like most large families. I think it still is like that. This is probably important for bonding with people. Obviously, you see some stereotypes in such families. I think I witnessed quite a few.

Indeed, while getting into the community I met plenty of characters...

The clever emo-goth cousin wearing only leather and weird boots. You don't always feel comfortable with him since you're not sure how he is going to react when you might point out something flawed he did. He also tends to express weird and offensive opinions in public just for the sake of it.

The aunt you admire hoping to be one day a bit like her. The clearly inspiring person that takes you under her wing with great pleasure. If you pay attention you will likely get insights from her wisdom. You might not understand it at the time to only realize its significance later.

The uncle you like to tag along with because you know the time spent will be fun and crazy. He gets you to places you would never go to (karaoke bars anyone?) and do crazy things, like talking to drunken strangers in a foreign town.

The grandpa who is a great story teller. You always love spending time with him late during family reunions. When the great noisy time is over, he is still around gently telling real (or made up) stories.

The grandma who has lived several lives. Clearly you can gain wisdom from her experiences. That said, you also get the feeling that sometimes she is getting overly conservative and over-protective.

As a long timer, I also ended up in the oldies group, which gives you a whole new perspective...

Two sisters you appreciated, who had stopped talking to each other because of some feud. There might have been some valid reason years ago. Unfortunately, years after instead of being put to rest, one is estranged and some relationships in the family are still tainted by it.

The little cousin with attention deficit disorder who brings plenty of new activity ideas for the whole family, but rarely delivers completely and someone else picks up to complete his vision.

The little brother still trying to find his place in the family. He is still feeling insecure, but in time he'll grab the torch and move the family forward together with his whole generation. It is a privilege to see him grow.

Of course, there are many more such characters in our community and that is what makes it interesting and unfortunately I can't list them all here. My hope is that by pointing a few out bluntly it'll help members to reflect on their peers and try to improve how the family works so that it is rarely dysfunctional.

Conclusion

Yes, I do have a life and it involves all of the KDE family characters in some twisted way. This is not the kind of thing you really think about as a child. You don't envision something quite like it. But it happens. Most of us start because of some itch to scratch or technical curiosity, this is hardly a rational choice in the first place.

Similarly, I'll slightly change Desmond Tutu's words: "You don't choose your family. They are [the Universe's] gift to you, as you are to them."

Clearly, KDE has been a gift to me, a second family. This is why, just like for my first family, I try to be available for fellow gearheads and be a gift to them.

11 Deals with the Devil

Boudhayan Gupta

Some would say his childhood was misspent, but when you a put a computer, a CD with a Linux distribution, and the permission to do anything one pleases with the two in front of a 13-year old boy, there's only one way it can end. After acquiring ninja Linux skills, picking up a couple of programming languages, and enrolling for an undergraduate course in Computer Science and Engineering, Boudhayan Gupta broke into the KDE Community in early 2015, eager to help in the ongoing effort to port software to KDE Frameworks 5. Today, he maintains KDE's screenshot utility, is a system administrator, and a member of KDE e.V.. In the very rare few moments when he's not studying or devoting time to KDE, he can be seen trying to learn as many languages and read as many books as he possibly can.

It is the middle of autumn, almost exactly nineteen years to the day KDE was born. An e-mail has just been posted to the community mailing list. The e-mail is barely 20 lines long, and contains a very simple suggestion. Over the course of two months, this thread will grow to over two hundred e-mails, split itself into multiple threads across three mailing lists, with nearly a hundred people participating, putting on clear public display the passion the people have for not just what KDE builds, but what the community stands for. This debate and the resulting action will lay down precedent for services the community will offer to its members in the future. This is the story of what happened, and how it changed our community for the better.

Free Software Isn't Just About Freedom

Free software is about freedom; that is what the free stands for. Free software isn't gratis software, it's libre software. But free software isn't as much about freedom as it is about control, and making sure that that control remains with the widest possible populace. Free software abhors any action whose possible consequences include loss of control over the software by any member who currently has it. In the context of free software, we can define freedom in terms of the control the users of the software has over how they use it, with whom they share it, and how they change it. The KDE Community recognizes that simply making sure users have control over how the software is used, modified and shared isn't enough to guarantee a healthy ecosystem fostering the development and use of free software. Like the users, contributors must also be guaranteed certain freedoms, defined in terms of control over how they contribute to the project. The contributors dictate how they want to develop the software; the kind of tooling they want to use, the kind of workflows they want to maintain, and the ways in which they communicate, among others. To guarantee these freedoms to the developers, the community must do everything in their power to ensure control over our infrastructure ultimately remains in the hands of the contributors.

The KDE System Administrators

The KDE System Administrators (whom we really should call Infrastructure Engineers, since that describes their role more accurately) are responsible for maintaining the infrastructure that supports the activities of the community. This extends to beyond supporting the development of software. A considerable chunk of the infrastructure exists to provide spaces for people to collaborate on tasks of any sort, be it administrative, financial, or related to development. The KDE System Administrators exist to meet the technical needs of the community. To ensure that it does always meet the needs of the community, the system administrators need to ensure that they never find themselves in a position where they are unable to provide what the community requires, because services provided by other providers which the community relies on do not let us do things we need to do. This is why we host our own source code management servers instead of relying on one of the large proprietary hosted services. We simply cannot let other service providers dictate what we are allowed to do with our infrastructure. This example is pertinent because of the subject matter of the aforementioned email thread. The email thread was a request from an active developer asking for the presence of KDE's code repositories on GitHub.

KDE on GitHub

It was clear from the very beginning that hosting our repositories on GitHub and having all our activity take place there would not be tenable, because of the loss of control over our infrastructure that would entail. Among other things, we wouldn't be able to ensure:

1. The availability of code hosting and code review services, as if GitHub decides to change their services, for technical or financial reasons, and their services are no longer in line with our technical or financial requirements, we would find ourselves without a place to publicly host our code, and coordinate our development activities.

2. The integrity of the code repositories, since a breach in their security would allow code in the repositories to be altered. While our own infrastructure is also susceptible to such a problem, if such an incident happens on our own infrastructure, the accountability is shared by the community and getting recourse is infinitely easier. Our response to such an incident would be tailored to our needs, which cannot be guaranteed for a hosted service.

At the same time, the code being present on GitHub has distinct practical advantages. Some of the more important ones include:

1. Code visibility. A vast number of people who are just beginning their journeys in the world of open source software are simply not aware that open source code exists outside of GitHub, thanks to the brilliant publicity and ubiquity GitHub has achieved. Having code available on GitHub would ensure the code will be discoverable by such people.

2. Developers' credibility. A lot of employers simply look at a person's GitHub profile to find a prospective employee's publicly available code, and evaluate their suitability for the job. Having KDE's code on GitHub, with the commits made by a developer showing up in their profile would make a vast amount of code available for these prospective employers to peruse, as well as display the developer's ability to cooperate with other developers and contribute to a shared codebase.

3. An offsite hot spare. If KDE's infrastructure were ever to go down, having our code on GitHub would ensure that the code would continue to remain accessible while we work to bring our services back online. Also, since it is possible to clone a repository from GitHub and push new commits to our infrastructure, this would lessen some of the load on our systems.

Eventually, a solution was found. GitHub has a feature wherein organizations are able to host mirrors of their own self-hosted Git repositories on GitHub, which we would make use of. These mirrors can be made read-only, and all extra features of GitHub (such as the wiki, the bug tracker, etc) can be disabled for these repositories. All the KDE System Administrators would need to do is to push new commits from our master Git server to GitHub, in addition to our own read-only mirror network. It took us a month since the first e-mail[1] was sent to decide to have the mirror set up, but the actual

---

[1] https://mail.kde.org/pipermail/kde-community/2015q3/001507.html

work was conducted over a 36 hour period between September 16 to September 18, 2015. First, we realized that the URL github.com/kde was already in use by a user who had no activity, and therefore our first task was to liaise with GitHub and get the organization assigned to us[2]. Then I got to work cooking up the scripts that would push the repositories we wanted to our new shiny GitHub organization. On September 17th, I finished up that work and handed the scripts over to the Git infrastructure maintainer. As I went to sleep in India, he woke up in New Zealand, reviewed the scripts and added them to those we already ran when new commits were pushed to our master server. On the 18th, we were able to announce to the world that KDE was now present on GitHub[3]. The discussions on the mailing lists continued, and we reached a few ideological conclusions regarding how we would engage with proprietary hosted services outside our control. We concluded that for practical reasons we could never shut them out, but that we should never rely on these services to fulfill our core requirements. Additionally, we concluded that we should always work towards bringing people on these hosted services to our own infrastructure.

KDE on Telegram

The KDE Community has always relied on IRC (Internet Relay Chat) to provide online chat rooms where people can get together and discuss development. IRC has developed a subculture, and people hang out in IRC channels to meet new people, socialize online and discuss as much off-topic content as on-topic content. IRC has a special place in the hearts of seasoned people in the open source world. It is interesting to note that with all the care that we take to retain control over every bit of our infrastructure, we don't actually host our IRC services ourselves, instead delegating it to Freenode, a community run by people with strong ideological ties to the free

---

[2]https://mail.kde.org/pipermail/kde-community/2015q3/001704.html
[3]https://mail.kde.org/pipermail/kde-community/2015q3/001717.html

software culture, many of whom are also associated with the KDE Community. It is one of the very few cases where we can trust an external provider to host services for us. During the preparations for our annual mentoring program in 2016, we realized that there was an entirely disjoint set of people who were active participants in the KDE Community, but had never ever used our IRC services, and were therefore invisible to the people who regularly used IRC to keep in touch with their friends in the community. Part of a generation of people never exposed to the wonders of IRC, instead, these people used Telegram, a service that provides encrypted one-on-one and group messaging services. Telegram has apps on mobile phones, all major desktop operating systems (including GNU/Linux), and a very functional website to fall back to if all else fails. Unlike IRC, which uses its own ports (which may be blocked at workplaces and universities) and requires dedicated clients, Telegram simply works over encrypted HTTP, over standard HTTP ports, and simply requires a web browser to function. Telegram allows the transfer of images and files, has native support for emoticons and "stickers", and works on the go with their lightweight mobile apps. There is only one problem with Telegram: it is run by a for-profit entity whose interests may not always be in line with KDE's. While we could never officially endorse the use of Telegram, with the precedent set by having our repositories hosted on GitHub, we could extend our support to people using the service. Telegram users also being active participants in the KDE Community, we owe it to them to make it feasible for them to participate in discussions happening on the IRC channels. We also owe it to our IRC users to be able to join discussions happening on Telegram. The solution to this was simple. We used one of our servers to run a bot. This bot would read messages from an IRC channel and post the same messages on the Telegram group. It would also read messages from the Telegram group and post them on the IRC channel. This way, Telegram users keep themselves abreast of the conversation happening on IRC, and IRC people get to participate in the discussion happening on Telegram. Everyone is happy.

A Happy Ending

In some countries, KDE is still not old enough to be of legal drinking age. Over its 20 years of existence, the community has learned lessons, and incorporated these lessons into their way of conducting their activities. There were important lessons learned from these two experiences. Firstly, with a community this large, there is always going to be a difference of opinion, and some of these opinions may be incompatible with each other. Pleasing everyone is impossible, but there is always a compromise to be found for people who are willing to find it. Secondly, shutting users of proprietary systems and services out is never an option. Trying to find a solution that would enable such users to use our services and participate in our community is the only responsible thing to do. Finally, KDE is as much a sociopolitical movement as it is a group of technical geniuses building great software, and it shows. KDE is what it is because of the people; people who have poured their heart and soul into the community and the software, and who voluntarily take ownership of the community's positions and actions, products and activities. The political and social stands the community takes on issues is its identity, and forms the basis for commanding the respect it deserves. KDE is now 20 years old, and the community is primed to make itself grow for 20 more years, and then 20 more after that. If there is anything we can be sure of, it is that experiences like this will continue to happen, and such stories will continue to be written.

12 Defining a Vision and Mission for KDE

Thomas Pfeiffer

Thomas Pfeiffer is mainly responsible for usability matters within KDE's Visual Design Group, where he works to keep developers, designers and his fellow usability professionals focused on our common goal: Creating the best possible experience for our users! Recently, he has taken up an additional focus: Trying to move KDE forward as a community, both in terms of helping us find a direction and in terms of communicating with the outside world.

In spring 2015, Lydia Pintscher started the initiative "Evolving KDE" with the goal of "helping KDE and KDE e.V. get a better understanding of where we are, where we want to go and how we want to get there". One of the central actions of this initiative was to run a survey asking members of the KDE Community why they are a part of it, what they want to achieve and what they think is currently missing.

One important result of that survey was that many in the community felt a lack of a common Vision driving KDE forward. To fix that, a group of people formed during Akademy to write a Vision draft for KDE. The team collected a lot of ideas and went through several iterations of a Vision draft. However, around the end of the year, the process was stuck. The team was unsure about the scope the Vision should have (should they immediately go for a Vision for all of KDE or start with one for the KDE e.V. first?) and whether the whole community could ever agree on a single Vision in the first place.

Andrew Lake, who had supported the team with his experience in Vision creation, had just started a new, very demanding job and could not find the time to drive the project forward anymore. Since

I was still convinced that a Vision was crucial for KDE, I took over that support role. Discussions with the team showed that at first, we had to decide whether we want a Vision or a Mission for KDE. In the end, we decided that we needed both: A Vision to define what we want the future to be like, and a Mission to determine how we want to get there.

With that settled, we agreed on a first draft for a Vision and opened the discussion with the rest of the community. Pretty quickly, two groups formed within those joining the discussion: One group (which included the original drafting group) wanted the Vision to focus more on overarching goals like freedom and privacy for software users. The other group wanted the Vision to focus more on practical aspects like client software written in Qt, and created a counter-proposal to our Vision draft.

After long and heated debates and more and more tension building up between the two groups, we came to a realization: The world we wanted to live in was actually the same, what we disagreed on was just how to get there. With that realization, we decided that we should postpone the debate about the means for the moment, and first express our shared goals.

From this point on, it all went much easier, and after a few more iterations, the discussion converged onto a Vision which everyone who participated in the discussion agreed with: What KDE wants is

> A world in which everyone has control over their digital
> life and enjoys freedom and privacy.

Glad that we had put our differences behind us for the moment, we published our Vision. The article with which we published it already hinted at the next step that we'd need to take: Writing a Mission statement describing how we want to work towards our Vision.

The Vision as such was received very positively, but since it is - purposefully - vague, people were eager to know what it means in practice. To answer that question, we set out to create a Mission statement. Since we had merely postponed discussing the differences in the community regarding the "how" to the Mission discussion, I had feared that these differences would now bubble up again. To my surprise, this did not really happen. It turned out that once we had agreed on the "what", when it came to the "how", the differences were not as big as we expected. We agreed on many aspects of our Mission, yet there were many important details where we disagreed. The problem was that far fewer people participated in the Mission discussion than in the Vision discussion during its most active phase.

In the end, the differences often boiled down to "your opinion against mine". Since individual opinions can hardly be a good basis for a Mission which guides a whole community, I wanted to give everyone in the community a chance to voice their opinion on the points we already agreed on, and especially on the ones which were still debated, so I did what more then a decade of research training and experience had taught me: I set up an online survey. Since the Mission has to come from the community, of course that was the main target population for the survey. I also opened the survey to the outside world (capturing for each participant whether they are users of KDE software or active contributors to KDE), however, so that we can also see whether the community's priorities align with our users'.

Now we have 200 responses from (current or former) contributors, and almost 1200 responses from users, so we have a pretty good picture of what is important to both the contributors and interested users.

When the results are analyzed, they will feed back into our Mission statement which we want to have published well before QtCon in the beginning of September.

In the meantime, it delights me to see that the Vision is already used in practice: KDE contributors as well as users have used it on various occasions to remind us of the values that KDE stands for, which is exactly the purpose of a Vision. Especially the aspects of control and privacy seem to be of most importance to those who quote the Vision.

One way we aim to give users control is through our design mantra "Simple by default, powerful when needed": In order to make users feel in control of an application or a desktop environment, it has to be simple on the surface to not overwhelm them, but it has to provide them with the necessary features and configurability to still keep them in control even in more complex tasks. This is why, when people (users or contributors) use the Vision to justify an advanced feature or configuration option in a piece of KDE software, we as designers have to make sure that this is possible without any negative impact on the simplicity of the default experience.

The privacy aspect is equally important: Even though Free Software is generally more trusted to respect its users' privacy than proprietary software, it does not guarantee that automatically. Often data needs to be sent over the internet for a software to function, and sometimes we want to collect some data to for example know how many users we have. Our Vision does not forbid us to send or collect data, but it reminds us that we must always make sure that we do so only when necessary and only with the user's consent. I remember two examples of where the Vision was used to remind us of privacy as a goal: One was when a user noted that KMail was writing more information than necessary into email headers, for example the User-Agent header containing the version number of KMail and KDE Frameworks used, as well as the full uname string, which for most Linux distributions reveals both the kernel version and distribution used. Although putting such information in the User-Agent header is not uncommon among email clients, it would indeed be in line with our Vision if our client did not reveal any unnecessary information about the user's system. The other occasion when the Vision was used as an argument was in a discussion about KDE neon wanting to send the machine ID to our servers during software updates in order to allow them to count the number of active neon installations. This was discussed quite extensively, because while everyone agreed that it makes sense to count the number of active installations, it would theoretically allow us to connect the information that someone is using neon with other information connected with the same machine ID. In the end, what we agreed on as a minimum standard was clearly informing users about this data collection before they download a neon ISO, along with explaining to them how to disable such collection. The neon team plans to explicitly ask users to allow this data collection during the installation process in the future.

These very practical examples show that our Vision is not just empty words, but can already guide us in very fundamental questions. Even though the road to the Vision was rocky, this shows that the result was worth the effort!

13 On Subtle Contributions

Sandro Andrade

Sandro Andrade has been using Qt and KDE technologies since 2000, when he found a new tool to create amazing C++ visual applications – KDevelop. Sandro is one of the leading contributors to activities which have been fostering KDE in Brazil and South America, such as the creation of the Latin-America KDE Summit (LaKademy) in 2010. He was a member of the KDE e.V. Marketing Working Group, is the creator and maintainer of Minuet (the KDE-edu software for music education) and is currently a member of the KDE e.V. Board of Directors. Sandro holds a PhD in Computer Science and works as a professor in the Computer Science Department at IFBA, Brazil.

All of us want to see our beloved free software project succeed. Indeed, we do a lot of consciously planned work to achieve such a freedom nirvana. We strive to come up with a nice idea, decide about promising technologies to adopt, and code hopelessly to have an initial release to show off and maybe herd some new users and contributors around the world. If you deliver your software as part of a well-established and large community such as KDE, a brave army of translators, designers, testers, sysadmins, packagers, and promo people is promptly put in place to provide you all the needed support.

From the end-user perspective, only a small portion of such a huge effort becomes effectively apparent, in the form of graphical interfaces, user documentation, helpful features, and so on. As you get more involved in the community and start delighting the full FLOSS experience, all those multifaceted contributions from different people start to become apparent and you are immediately snatched up with an irrevocable desire of saying a huge "Thank you" to all those contributors. That said, I would like to talk herein about a different sort of contribution though: the subtle contribution.

I started pushing KDE forward in Brazil in 2008 along with Tomaz Canabrava, when we presented a Qt short-course in one of the biggest Brazilian FLOSS conferences. At that time, only three Brazilian contributors were doing some nice but somehow stand-offish work related to development, translation, and packaging. In 2010 – as a result of many activities we did in 2009 at some universities and local FLOSS events – we witnessed the dawn of Akademy-BR, the first Brazilian KDE sprint ever and expanded it to the Latin-America KDE Summit (LaKademy) two years later, in 2012.

Nowadays, the Latin-American KDE contributor base is formed by 22 volunteers from Argentina, Brazil, Colombia, and Peru; working on activities related to development, translation, promotion, sysadmin, and artwork. After nearly nine years promoting KDE, doing some development and artwork contributions, and lately working on the overall community management, I now wonder what is that essential element that bonds people together, cultivates a thriving atmosphere, and makes such an odyssey last for 20 years.

People bond with each other by affinity. In FLOSS communities, more often than not, they bond by technological affinity, common interests in some application domain, or reciprocal wish to share knowledge. Whilst such coalescence factors are certainly quite important to build solid and healthy communities, I'd like to emphasize the importance of contributions that go readily unnoticed and, in spite of such contributor's unawareness, play a definite role when forging FLOSS communities. Failing to recognize such 'subtle contributions' not only hampers the catalysis of community growing but also lets 'subtle contributors' in the unknown about their own importance for the whole FLOSS ecosystem.

The first kind of subtle contribution I want to describe is 'people as extrinsic motivation'. Although I had been using Qt and KDE technologies for seven years already, it was only in 2008 when I and Tomaz had a conversation which ended with a "do you want to do that?", "if you want to do that, I also want to do it", "cool, let's do it". For some people, making things alone may be extremely troublesome. Having someone just to say "you can!" or even walk the path alongside you is one of the most beautiful subtle contributions I have ever seen.

Another subtle contribution is made by people able to proactively identify the small things that engender a welcoming and relaxed atmosphere. And that includes everything someone involved with coding, testing, translation, infrastructure, and packaging usually isn't able to identify, let alone execute. I am writing this book chapter in a hotel room in Porto Alegre (south Brazil), on the very last day of the 17th International Free Software Forum (FISL), where KDE took up an amazing booth, presented a whole day of nice talks, and celebrated its 20th anniversary. What a nice demonstration of subtle contributions!

Do you know that invigorating thrill and fond memories when a FLOSS meeting or sprint comes to its end? New features, bug fixes, and translations are awesome but I'd risk to say such a nirvana is primarily caused by a different stimulus. Subtle contributors turn us into a family. They care about how to decorate our booth, they come up with a big commemorative cake, they talk about life or they do not even need to talk to let us know they are quite comfortable and happy in being part of KDE.

I regret not being sensitive enough to realize KDE is a stronghold of subtle contributors earlier. I would have said more 'Thank you's.

14 The Importance of Face-To-Face Meetings

Dani Gutiérrez Porset

Dani Gutiérrez Porset is a Free Software activist. He does consulting around Free Software and teaches at the Public University of the Basque Country. He was a project manager at the Office for Free Software at the Basque Government. He organized Akademy-es in 2010 and 2013 as well as Akademy and the Qt Contributors' Summit in 2013.

When speaking about personal fulfillments, some of the best achievements reached by individuals and groups happen in environments where motivation is not tied to economic incomes but contribution to community, be it a big or a small one. Think about situations related to friendship, family or love. Or, beyond feelings, about an important discovery for human health.

In the subset of free software world that is formed by communities like KDE, what moves people to contribute with personal time (coding, designing, teaching, evangelizing and more) is not so much a possible chance of making business, but other factors like building a high quality product/service on your own or maybe with other colleagues, and of course sharing part of your "brain" around the world, like when you know that your program is being used in more than 50 countries.

Twenty years ago it was very hard to believe that a KDE code would be used in a place like a particle accelerator at CERN, or that a free software kernel would conquer the market of mobile devices. And these kinds of successes have been achieved not just by the contribution of hundreds, thousands of people, but also by means of a political point of view based on generosity and freedom to learn, modify and improve what past generations have been building for future generations, trying to create a better world.

Does this all mean that making money from free software is bad? Not at all. Today more and more companies are making good business thanks to open source components. Think about the many companies earning money thanks to Apache, Qt or Ruby on Rails. Free software companies have some interesting sides: it is expected that they make good products because of their "professionality", and they spread a fresh and competitive option among the traditional private market. But there is a but: in general it will be more difficult for companies to be open and share its software completely, because their spirit and deep motivation is mainly business-focused. And, again, it is not a bad thing (but a necessary one) that people do work for a living, or even to become rich.

Joining all of this with the field of politics, it would be great if there were a kind of basic income, publicly assured, for those people that during some part of their life dedicate themselves to produce and spread free software, in order to recognize its contribution to the world.

Among distinct useful tasks related to free software communities, typically we hear some like coding, designing, documenting and perhaps lawyering. But "free software communities" is three words and the last one means people cooperating together.

As we belong to the IT field, the interconnnection between our people is usually done remotely, with email, messaging, social networks, or video conferences on PCs, laptops, tablets or mobile phones. But no technology comes near the direct face-to-face encounter and its results. It is really great to meet us for the first time or even more when we have met before. It's interesting because we know each other not only from the techie side, but also regarding other important parts of our lives. And when we see and hear each other, and share a drink and laugh, and we realize our common target across the free software world, we come back home more motivated to go on working hard.

So, to create spaces where programmers, managers, designers,... meet face-to-face is key for a better continuation of the community. And a big opportunity to reach this "community empowerment" are the international meetings like Akademy or FOSDEM. For this reason, for the KDE Community it is a must to organize good Akademy encounters, mainly the technical part but also the casual and friendly one. Let's remain a community where we take care of all people who belong to it.

15 Remote Places Make Magic Possible

Mario Fux

Mario Fux is the father of two sons, husband, teacher, webmaster and a reader of almost anything. He is using Free Software for nearly 20 years and joined KDE around 2007. He is the main organizer of the annual Randa meetings - KDE's week-long tech summit - and helps where help is needed.

KDE was born twenty years ago, in the last millennium. Back then, I didn't know about it and its great and welcoming community. Back then I made my first experiences with GNU, Linux and distributions and thus Free Software in general. I think it was my first distribution, SuSE 5.3, that introduced me to KDE. KDE 0.9 or 1.X, I can't remember because I didn't stick to Linux at first but went back to Windows or maybe dual-booted. But something made me stick to the Free Software world and when people asked me about why I spent so much time on something I didn't earn any money from, and would spend hours or even days siting in front of a PC, I told them: "It's because everybody told me that you don't even get kicked for free these days, but here I found something where people are working on something in their spare time, because they love it with passion and this something even challenges multi-billion IT-businesses en passant."

So the Free Software movement became a big hobby of mine or better say, a big part of my life. I visited several Linuxtage in Germany, other Linux events abroad and then in 2007 Anne-Marie Mahfouf invited me to Akademy in Glasgow, Scotland. She is of course famous for her work in KDE Edu but we knew each other from a monthly column I wrote about Free Software in education: TUX&GNU@school. Around this time I was really active in the area of Free Software in education as I was a trained primary school teacher. I gave a presentation about my local school that I migrated to GNU/Linux and KDE software including old Windows education software under Wine. It was a very interesting week and although I was (and probably still am) quite shy I made some new contacts.

Back in Switzerland where I grew up and still live, my first Akademy experience began to affect me. I began to use more and more KDE software, and started to study computer sciences as my minor. I realized that I love to write code but it is not my biggest strength or talent. So how could I give back something to this community that offered me software I use daily for free and with pleasure? In the Free Software media I read about KDE sprints that happened frequently and there it was: the idea to host such a sprint. It was around the time that Aaron Seigo, one of the central people in KDE at the time, was in Zurich for a presentation. I studied there and thus could visit his presentation and used the opportunity to tell him about my idea and that I would invite him and the other Plasma hackers to come to Randa where I would offer them a place to sleep, electricity, some internet connectivity and a beautiful and distraction-free surroundings, and inspiring nature.

In August 2009 it really happened: more than 15 women and men hackers from around the world arrived in a village with a population of less than 400 people in the middle of nowhere. They all arrived safely at my parent's Chalet (local holiday house) and although I didn't know them the Plasma team felt like family immediately. For a week they hacked, discussed, hiked and wrote software that I and millions of other people use and even better: can and will use in the future.

It was an amazing week for everybody and it just couldn't stop there. We needed to find a bigger house for more people. And there is a bigger house in town; actually the biggest house in Randa that we rent since 2010 for one week a year. That's the story of how the Randa Meetings were born.

(Almost) every year since 2009 several dozen Free Software enthusiasts come to Randa and spend a week eating, sleeping, discussing, hacking, deciding and contributing under one roof. This wouldn't be possible without the help and support of a lot of other people: my wife, children, parents, brother and even my aunts and uncles are helping. And there are a lot of Free Software people not part of my family that help as well. It's a lot of work, a lot of joy and always great to see what can be achieved in one week with focus.

Over the years we saw important decisions made in Randa like at the Platform 11 discussion which led to the successful KDE Frameworks 5 releases. The KDE Multimedia team prepared some great Amarok releases in Randa and discussed with Qt the future of Phonon. Kdenlive, one of the best video editors in the world, not just in Free software, had some important meetings in the middle of the Swiss Alps and decided to formally become part of the KDE community. The KDE Education group worked tirelessly in Randa days and long nights and now includes GCompris, which has been ported from Gtk to Qt, and has become part of the KDE community. And in recent years we worked hard to bring KDE software to new devices and even proprietary platforms as I strongly believe that even users of proprietary operating systems should be able to use our great software and thus know about us and be able to support us.

Although I strongly believe in the values of a Free operating system and will most probably always use one of them on my main systems I think that we should bring our values and software to other systems as well. And we should not be afraid of asking for money, either. The most important software distribution channels now are the Google Play Store and the Apple Store and I'm convinced that KDE should be there. Actually we are already there - some of ours apps are included and downloadable for millions of users. But let's ask them for a Franken, Dollar or Euro or two and we'll get the money and can use it to support development.

Back to the farther future of KDE. I'm sure we will still be active and healthy in five, ten and then twenty years and I hope that the Randa Meetings will be there too. It would be great if at least one of my kids would still be involved in these great meet-ups in the middle of Europe. And if I had a wish for KDE I'd say KDE should become more self-confident; we have such great software and values. More people should know and use our software, and embrace our values. If we stay such a welcoming community and continue to open up in areas like promotion, artwork, design and communication, we'll become even more successful. As we become even more international, more people on this planet will know about our great projects and use our software and thus become part of this great community.

About the first train that drove through the Matter Valley, where Randa is located, 125 years ago, it was said: "Great people create great things, but good people create the perpetual." KDE people are good people, creating for the future.

16 KDE in Taiwan

Franklin Weng

Franklin Weng is open source developer, translator and promoter from Taiwan. He is the coordinator of KDE's zh_TW translation team since 2006 and the president of the Software Liberty Association Taiwan.

I'm a maverick. I've always been one. Well, okay, to some extent. When I completed graduate school in 1999, my classmates rushed to the Hsinchu Science Park to find a high-pay job at TSMC or UMC. I didn't. I went to a small company outside the Hsinchu Science Park. That company was developing their own search engine at that time, and I was their 19th employee.

While my colleagues were using Windows 98 and NT 3.0, I was using Red Hat 7.2 with Chinese Linux Extension, and KDE/GNOME as my desktop system. At that time, I wasn't bound to a specific desktop system. I started with KDE, then jumped to GNOME due to the beauty of Gaelon. No matter what desktop system I used, I kept looking for a useful mail client.

The first mail client I was satisfied with and started translating was Sylpheed, which was developed by a Japanese developer and based on GTK. Sylpheed was good, but at that time it couldn't dock into my system tray in GNOME. I used GNOME and Sylpheed for some years, but eventually tried KDE again for KMail because it could dock in the system tray in KDE. It was that simple, and since then I have been bound to KDE.

My first impression was that KDE was beautiful. KDE had abundant software for all kinds of jobs to use. KDE had many cool effects. I loved it, and I started to translate for it, starting with KMail, and then contributing to many other applications. I was proud to be the only one in my company who fully used Linux and KDE as my daily work environment. I was also proud to contribute to the traditional Chinese translations of KDE, even though I was the only one to do this.

Then KDE 4 was released. I had not yet changed my desktop to 4.0, but I had introduced FOSS and KDE 4.0 in some talk I gave around that time. KDE 4 was buggy, but it still gave me a lot of fun. When KDE 4.1 was released, I fell in love with KDE all over again and changed my daily work environment to KDE 4.1 almost immediately. I still remember the moment I understood the concept of Plasma. It was when I successfully put the application menu on the desktop, instead of the panel. It is a bit silly, but I was quite excited when I realized this.

In 2012 I successfully changed the default desktop environment in EzGo to Plasma 4. EzGo is a derived Linux distribution used to promote FOSS in Taiwan's school. The main reason to change to Plasma was because it still had an application menu while the other desktop environments had removed theirs. We had some (well, a lot of) arguments about this change, but we finally decided to use Plasma 4. Then, in 2013 we successfully "defeated" Microsoft and managed to install Linux and Plasma 4 on the 10,000 computers New Taipei City purchased that year. I also created some Debian packages so that we could easily change Kubuntu into EzGo.

KDE is no longer a mere desktop system but a community of people dedicated to creating a free and user-friendly computing experience, offering an advanced graphical desktop, a wide variety of applications for communication, work, education and entertainment and a platform to easily build new applications upon. However, I have no idea how many people are aware of the change from a desktop-centric system to a set of people dedicated to creating beautiful experiences in the world of FOSS. Maybe most people seem to still treat KDE as a desktop system only. Maybe.

KDE is facing a crisis of identity. After the iPad was born, the computing world was flipped on its head. The famous vision for "a computer on every desk" is almost realized. Facing such a huge change, what is in the future for KDE? I see that many old communities like GNOME or Mozilla are facing these same challenges. We all need to change, no doubt. IMHO, KDE must keep its identity while adapting into the current new digital world. KDE should use its advantages of being based on Qt and aim for being ported to Android and iOS. KDE has many good applications that could be used on Android or iOS with some user interface changes. At the same time, it should not be too difficult to keep maintaining software on the older platforms like PC and laptops. Even so, the marketing part of KDE can and should aim to be more compact and effective.

I'm always proud to be a member of KDE. Let's make it better.

17 Building KDE's Community in India

Pradeepto Bhattacharya

Pradeepto Bhattacharya started contributing to KDE in 2005. He started with KDE promotion in India and then contributed to KDE PIM for a few years. He founded the KDE India community and has served on KDE e.V.'s Board of Directors. He lives in Pune, India with his wife. He works for Red Hat in the Developer Tools Engineering Group.

In March 2016, the KDE India community organized its 5th edition of conf.kde.in, the annual Qt/KDE conference in India, in Jaipur. Jaipur is a small laid-back city in the North West part of India. It took 10 years for KDE India to reach Jaipur. This essay tries to tell you that story briefly, the 10 years of KDE's journey in India, a sub-set of its own 20 years journey. A story in which many new friends were made who came together at different points of time to make this journey a very happy memory.

It started with a Birds of Feather session at FOSS.IN, at that point India's and perhaps Asia's largest Open Source conference, on December 2nd 2005. Two KDE developers, Till Adam and Sirtaj Singh Kang (Taj), were participating in the conference. I had flown down to Bangalore from Mumbai to attend my first ever Open Source conference. I used to write Qt code for a company in Mumbai and eagerly wanted to know what all this Open Source is about. The result of the BoF session was the founding of an informal group called KDE India. Very simple beginnings - a mailing list for the Indian community and a sub-domain in.kde.org because somebody owned kde.in already. Some time later, when that domain was available, KDE e.V took it under its wings. Aaron Seigo was supposed to attend the conference as well but he couldn't because of another clashing conference. He made it up by coming to India for FOSS.IN/2006.

After the conference in 2005, the community basically grew very slowly. I didn't let go of any speaking opportunity between 2006 and 2009. I went to any college or university or anyone organizing a FOSS event and would let me speak about KDE at their event. Thanks to Google Summer of Code and Season of KDE, we got a few KDE contributors from India over the next few years. Earliest contributors that I can remember were Sharan Rao, Piyush Verma, Akarsh Simha etc. I am fortunate to be still in touch with all of them. In 2007, the FOSS.IN organizers came up with a brilliant master stroke - "project days" for various Open Source projects. These were modeled around LCA mini-confs or FOSDEM rooms. We had to submit proposals even for "project days". KDE got a slot for a KDE Project Day. Long-time KDE contributors Kévin Ottens, Till Adam and Volker Krause all were present for the KDE Project Day and the main conference.

For any success story, there is always an inflection point. KDE India's story has one as well. It was in 2008. I contacted an acquaintance of mine, Madhusudhan CS, who was still an engineering student in Bangalore to help me with a certain idea for the KDE Project Day at FOSS.IN. I requested him to keep it a secret because I wasn't sure about the idea myself and how I would execute it. Anyway, Madhu seemed to be sold on the idea but he couldn't help himself from keeping the secret from his best friend and classmate Santosh Vattam. Both started helping with the idea the next day. As it turned out, Madhu and Santosh were excellent in selling the idea to their classmates and soon, I had a whole "secret" team - Krishna, Aditya - working on the idea. The idea was to create 1 or 2 KDE fliers and hand them out at the KDE Project Day. As it turned out, with the help of an excellent team, your idea can multiply manifold. The output wasn't just a couple of fliers but a complete booklet. The first KDE handbook was born. Soon we realized that we needed money to print the booklet and lots of it if we wanted to make it co lour and do it right. Taj came to rescue, he convinced his company to sponsor the complete costs - a princely sum of Rs.

40,000 - to get the book printed. Those booklets traveled to Jamaica, Nigeria, Europe, Malaysia, Taiwan and many other places.

The booklet wasn't the inflection point and Madhusudhan didn't just help me find volunteers for the project day. He also played the crucial role of introducing me to a junior student from his college - Shantanu Jha. That changed everything for KDE India and me. I finally found the guy who was crazier and better than I could ever dream of. It was the beginning of a great partnership for many years. I probably haven't trusted anyone as much in my life as Shantanu. Knowing that I could delegate work to him and it would get done was such a relief. With his help we kept organizing KDE Project Days and other co-opted events at various conferences across India. During this period, many contributors kept coming and going.

Shantanu followed the tradition of his mentors. He got more friends to contribute to KDE - Sinny (whom Shantanu married later), Sudhendhu. In March 2011, we organized the first conf.kde.in in Bangalore. A lot of sacrifices went into it by everyone. I don't think it would have been possible if anyone would have been missing in the team. A lot of new faces met for the first time - Vishesh, Rohan, Kunal, Smit etc. Since 2013, conf.kde.in has become an annual traveling event. The event has traveled from Bangalore to Gandhinagar to Kollam to Jaipur. After Bangalore in 2011, every year the event has been organized in a smaller city or town and it has always been organized in some university, a tradition that the Indian community has learned from Akademy.

In this past decade many people have played a crucial role in keeping the KDE Community up and running in India. Atul Chitnis, Kishore Bhargava, Tarique Sani, Swati Sani, Prashanth Udupa, Atul Jha, Sujith, Abhishek Patil, Supreeth Vattam, Kamal, Anurag, Aanjhan, Runa, Sankarshan, Kushal, Harish, Yash, Devaja, Akshay, Ashish, Shivam, Sagar. The list is long but not complete. Over the period of a decade, many KDE members from the US and Europe have visited India during the events and graced us with their knowledge and love. Adriaan de Groot, Sebastian Kügler, Lydia Pintscher,

Simon Hausmann, Frederik Gladhorn, Kenny Duffus, Jos Poortvliet and others - you all are a part of the KDE India family.

A community always needs fresh and young blood to keep going strong. Slowly but surely we see new members join the KDE India community. The community is small but it keeps going on. Bhushan, Boudhayan and others contribute to KDE and are role models for the future generations of KDE contributors in India. The KDE family is growing and I really hope it keeps going.

I have seen this community or should I say this family and its journey first hand through my eyes and I have been a part of it. I am extremely proud of it and I feel humbled that I have had the opportunity to meet such a great set of people from across my country and the whole world. I feel I am really fortunate that I am a part of this journey and this family.

18 A Revolution in Itself

Yash Shah

Yash Shah is an active contributor to KDE since 2011. He started his journey with contributing to the speech recognition program Simon through Google Summer of Code and then along with the KDE India team, he organized two of the largest KDE conferences in India - KDE Meetup 2013 and conf.kde.in 2014. He loves evangelizing KDE and motivating students to contribute to open source in different colleges in India.

One of the largest international open source conferences was organized in India: The KDE Meetup 2013 and conf.kde.in 2014 at Dhirubhai Ambani Institute of Information and Communication Technology (DA-IICT) in Gandhinagar, Gujarat. It was a platform for the exchange of ideas and thoughts with speakers coming from different cultures, leading to an advancement in the essence of open source development and reliving the joys of contributing in KDE. Both the events were a huge phenomenon in itself with the participation of over 350 students from the far ends of the country such as Delhi, Durgapur, Mumbai and many more.

It was always my dream to host something at a scale like this in Gujarat. People in our state were not aware of FOSS. With over 150 engineering colleges, there was a huge opportunity to introduce them to the world of contributing to FOSS. When my colleagues and I first started planning the event, we never imagined that we would receive so much support from across India and from around the world. We never thought in our wildest dreams that we might attract an amazing group of developers and open source enthusiasts from more than 9 states in India. Both conferences served for a perfect environment for getting people to know about KDE and open source software development in general. The expert KDE contributors flew in from different parts of India, Europe and USA to talk about KDE applications, introducing the audience to KDE and open source tools and technologies and answer their questions.

One thing that we experienced is that international conferences such as these serve as the perfect arena for students to get involved with open source and to get themselves acquainted with the way communities such as KDE function. These events are the perfect opportunity to interact with these mentors and members who can guide them along and also help them to participate in various coding mentoring programs such as Google Summer of Code and Season of KDE. Students get to collaborate with them and also build upon their own ideas and create new projects of their own as a part of KDE.

One of the major highlights of the event - the Bardoli incident - is an inspiration and an indication of the dedication of the members of the KDE Community to spread knowledge among all and to ensure that everyone is a part of the community and that no one feels left out. Many enthusiastic students from Bardoli sacrificed their weekend time off and came from far away places and were prepared to make the most of the event. Despite the long journey accompanied by fatigue, they did their best to work along with the speakers but somehow it did not work out for them and they decided to leave the event. Pradeepto saw them leaving and he sat with all of them and talked personally to each one of them. He convinced them to stay. The next day, special sessions were organized just for them and all of them showed up with renewed interest. They covered all that they had missed in a short span of time and were eager to learn more.

Let me share an insight to the positive things people consumed from the conference and how the talks changed their way of thinking. This was a text from a delegates of conf.kde.in who traveled 700km to attend it:

> Nobody cares about the people, only wants gathering and all. No one knows what were participants doing. But as

we cared a lot by you and your team is really appreciated. Thanks for my side behalf of all participant.
#kdemeetup One thing to learn.. Don't be scared of coding.[1]

At the end of the event there was a newfound inspiration in all the participants who had the desire to contribute and to be a part of the largest and friendliest community in the world. This was a change, a different sort of exposure which the students received which relieved them from the usual drudgery and boredom of college education which does not expose them to real-world programming. The event lived up to its aim - helping people know about KDE and to provide them with the basic skills and techniques so that they can contribute to open source. The community speakers were as warm and amiable as they could be and the students were encouraged to approach them and ask as many doubts as they could. This event left the students asking for more. All that they had in their minds was to learn and explore and innovate - create something which could be the next revolution. It gives us motivation to hold such kind of conferences at other places so that young students can benefit more than ever and the culture of FOSS keeps thriving in this world.

---

[1] https://mail.kde.org/pipermail/kde-india/2014-April/001236.html

19 Think Globally, Act Locally

Aleix Pol i Gonzàlez

Aleix Pol i Gonzàlez has been contributing to KDE since 2007. He started working in software development in the KDE Education area and on KDevelop. He was the president of KDE España from 2012 to 2016 as well as a founding member of the organization. Aleix joined the KDE e.V. board of directors in 2014. In his day-job, he is employed by BlueSystems where he has worked with other parts of the community including Plasma and Qt.

In KDE we are very proud of being a diverse community. We strive to make sure it is - it's not easy. Albeit being an international community it wouldn't take an anthropologist to look at the KDE Community and realize that although we are diverse we are not spread out evenly across the globe. Instead, we have some defined demographics around age, sex, studies and probably income as well. What I want to discuss today is one of my longstanding focuses since I joined KDE: local communities, or how to offer to my people what we create.

From a creator's perspective, it is useful to turn around and look at who we are dealing with. When it comes to a specific project, one thinks of rather stereotypical people who might be interested in IDEs or spreadsheets, but when we think about what we want to offer as a whole, I can't help but think of society in a whole different way. The further away you push it, the clearer it is that it is not about adding specific features, but about listening to what users need and explaining how we can solve the problems they see; to be there when they need assistance and to help them be secure rather than adventurous.

We created KDE España to be able to sustain Akademy-es (the KDE conference in Spain) initially, but over time it has evolved into a platform with a much broader communication spectrum including Akademy-es, a magnificent blog, podcasts, training materials and conferences. This is also important because as soon as you start communicating, people come to you when they feel unsure about how to help. Furthermore, it helps us stay organized and alive.

Interestingly, one of the initiatives we have started from within KDE España has been achieved by narrowing the geographical scope even further. We created a group called Barcelona Free Software, where we offer content from local free software experts and enthusiasts including but not limited to us. This allows people with different interests to those who would attend Akademy or Akademy-es, to come and talk to us. The feedback we get at such gatherings is interesting as it shows the kind of problems that our people ache from and how they ask for solutions.

In the end, what this experience has reminded me of is that I am here to make sure society can make the best use of the available technology. Furthermore, in a society increasingly based on information, we need to let it empower the user, the people. We need to remember what the advantages of offering free software solutions are beyond technologies, by remembering that the end goal is that people have the tools they need to create better content in every aspect of their lives, and that includes the possibility to adapt the tools they use.

I think one of the most important motivational factors is to see people being able to adopt the solutions you come up with, and another even more motivational factor is when they use them to create new things. For many of us, it is beyond the comfort zone or even the ideal plan for a weekend but it is worth it to talk to people, it is worth going to that local convention to talk about why and how important it is to grow our society on free software and then gather reasons why that is not the case yet. The response never ceases to amaze me.

20 A User at the Court of KDE Developers

Baltasar Ortega

Teacher by profession, Baltasar Ortega is a user who knows nothing about programming and who loves Free Software and the KDE Community. When he is not teaching in his school, he writes a popular blog about the KDE Community and its work (kdeblog.com). He is the secretary of and responsible for communication in KDE España.

This is the personal story of how a simple user has become a member of the KDE Community and the daily struggle for the success of a project you are passionate about.

This story is written to commemorate the 20 years of the KDE project which I consider extremely important for the development of software worldwide and in which I feel completely integrated. Sometimes I do not completely understand the language of the developers with whom I communicate almost on a daily basis, which sometimes makes me feel like an astronaut at the court of King Arthur.

It all started when, after many unsuccessful attempts and thanks to the help of the free software communities forums, I managed to configure a USB router to work with my newly installed GNU/Linux distribution. I think it was an openSUSE 10 and came with the KDE desktop. I simply gave my PC software that I thought is better. It started from selfishness.

At that time I did not completely grasp the workings of the ecosystem and its applications but I quickly realized that the KDE project gave me what I wanted: a nice configurable desktop, free from malware, 100% translated into my language and with convenient applications like Konqueror, Kontact, Kate, Amarok, Digikam, etc.

However KDE Software was just something that was "created out of nothing" and I used it without paying much attention to its origin.

Gradually I started to fall in love with KDE and eventually I realized that everyone should enjoy their computer as much as I was enjoying mine. Thus I was determined to help spreading the word about GNU/Linux and the KDE project but did not know how. I did not know how to code, I could not draw, I did not like to translate and did not know how to package software.

I, as a teacher, knew only how to explain things... so I created a blog about KDE: kdeblog.com, where I would try to help others get started in this wonderful world of ours.

Thanks to the blog I started learning a lot about the world of Free Software; making many mistakes along the way but always learning. This is how discovered that events were held regularly and discovered that there was a regional group for KDE: KDE España... then I applied to become a member... then I was accepted, surprisingly to me... then I decided to attend the annual meeting: Akademy-es 2010 in Bilbao. That meant traveling 600 km from where I live to an event where I knew no one except for a few email exchanges. It was the experience that definitely changed my view of Free Software.

They welcomed me as one of them and I discovered what KDE really is about. There I discovered that behind each application, each translation, each design on my computer there is a person who made it possible. There I discovered that these people have great ethical and moral values and there I discovered I wanted to be a part of this gear.

Suddenly it was no longer only KDE Software; KDE was a project of people making software for other people, respecting their freedoms and privacy. That was a great discovery for me, I wanted to be an active part of the KDE Community and help spread it.

I understood that the KDE Community consists of all kinds of people, not just coders as one could have assumed, and that myself as a user without any coding skills, could play an important role in the development of Free Software.

The rest, as they say, is history.

In that year I became "a user at the court of KDE Developers" working every day to promote Free Software from my particular point of view, either on the blog, in social networks, by giving talks, putting stickers on my computer, telling my students about the free alternatives, collaborating with projects such as Wikipedia or OpenStreetMaps, installing GNU/Linux on my friends' computers, organizing local events such as the 15th anniversary of KDE party or the Jornadas Libres de Vilareal - all without knowing how to write a single line of code.

A thank you comment, being able to travel, learning languages, learning new working methods and understanding that I am part of a community that works for the good of humanity, all this has given me great pleasure. But above all it has given me the opportunity to meet extraordinary people who devote so much time to creating a better world.

Finally, I want to thank all the people who have contributed, contribute and will contribute with all their work and their effort to keep the KDE Community active and thriving. It will always give you back more than you contribute.

21 Why I Chose KDE, and Why KDE Is Family

Valorie Zimmerman

Valorie Zimmerman has been using KDE software since the KDE 3 days. After meeting some KDE women in Linuxchix, she became active in Amarok documentation, then the Community Working Group, and also on the distribution level, the Kubuntu community. Valorie also helped build the Student Programs team, participating in the first Google Code-in for pre-college students, administering Season of KDE and Google Summer of Code. Building community is what it's all about.

Around 2001, my son showed me two desktops, and asked me to choose which one I wanted on my new install of Mandrake. I chose blue, the pretty one, and so began my KDE journey. Back then, I understood very little besides that I found KDE software to be not just more beautiful, but also usable and configurable.

Before contributing to KDE, life was busy with kids and work. Fortunately a friend introduced me to Linuxchix, so a friendly group who helped out newcomers welcomed me in. I met people who contributed all up and down the stack, including Windows users like me who were considering a move to Linux. So Linuxchix was my way in to KDE and Kubuntu.

Back in those KDE 3 days, KDE was still a bit controversial in free software circles. Qt licensing concerned some people and the KDE vs. GNOME rivalry seemed real and even upsetting to some advocates of free, libre software.

If any group wants to grow, it must have ways in. For KDE, I found IRC and mailing lists first. Many women on the internet find the hostility and bad behavior discouraging enough to never find their way in. Fortunately I had the Linuxchix at my back, and found KDE mostly welcoming. When I spoke up to volunteer, people enthusiastically replied, and gave me good suggestions about how to start. I found that every project needs better documentation! Growing groups will do everything they can to help you get started. I began in Amarok, which was such fun. After looking through old docs, and considering the options, we decided to do the Amarok Handbook on Userbase, KDE's user wiki. Not realizing that this was somewhat pioneering, we just plowed ahead, and used the old docs to make new pages in Userbase. It was great to work with Amarok developers, KDE documentation folks, along with the wonderful web team that has been keeping the wikis so useful to us.

A word on volunteering. Early in my "KDE career" I volunteered for the Community Working Group. Little did I know what I was getting into! That said, tackling the difficult issues between developers has been rewarding, because peace is usually the result. At the very worst, we know we tried our best to create a good situation out of a bad one. So blithely heading towards the cliff-edge like The Fool on the Tarot card, has been a good move. Getting to know people deeply is wonderful. Being a part of the Community Working Group has continually reminded me why KDE is family. Learning how to listen better, how to "fight fair", how to recognize issues as they are forming, and then helping them go in good directions, have made all of us involved better humans. I salute all the past, present and future members of the team, and peace-makers all around the world.

When the first Google Code-In was announced, those of us on the Amarok Handbook project immediately thought about all those unwritten pages, and began creating tasks for students; one task equaling one page. What a fantastic experience! It was wonderful to interact with those kids (ages 12-18) and help them help us. Once involved in Google Code-in, which was intense, exciting and productive, I was hooked on student programs in KDE. Looking back at the students who have worked with us over the years, one can see that student programs create the future of KDE. Our students begin working with mentors and teams, and our goal is always to welcome them into the family of KDE. Many of our most successful initiatives are now being run by former students, and many of our most effective mentors were once students themselves. Working with the Student Programs team has been so satisfying.

One of the things I love best about KDE is that while we do the inward-looking work, such as improving our processes, governance, and social relationships, we are generally outward looking. We don't simply make software that pleases us, but follow our ideals when working. I see developers write tests for their software even while complaining about how boring it is, simply because they value quality. I see people step up to write stories for KDE's official news site, release announcements and blog posts even when they dislike writing, because they want to share our work with the world. People comb the code for spelling errors and other small issues, and quietly fix them. Document writers do the same thing with the documentation – fix errors, test the texts to be sure they are up-to-date, contribute new screenshots – all quietly and often un-acknowledged. Our Visual Design Group created itself out of nothing, and quietly steps in to help application teams, Plasma developers, and web-workers. The Sysadmin team is tireless! They keep our infrastructure up, humming along happily, and most important: securely. They create new structures to help out the developers, and improve old ones. We have folks working upstream in Qt, making, for instance, accessibility Just Work for everyone. Our distributions are richer and healthier with KDE involvement, along with many other FOSS projects in the ecosystem that surrounds and supports us in turn.

All of this work affects all of us in KDE every day, but we may not notice it unless there is a problem. The focus on freedom and quality is now even moving onto platforms beyond Linux and BSD in a major way. Even folks who don't use Android, Mac or Windows have generously contributed to support developers making our applications usable to an even wider population. This generous spirit and welcoming attitude is what has kept me, a grandma, involved in creating KDE as long as I am able.

22 Story of a Contributor

Bhushan Shah

Bhushan Shah is an active contributor from India, previously a student of Information Technology, who started contributing to KDE two years ago. He maintains the flashable images for Plasma Mobile and is one of the administrators for KDE's mentoring programs.

I am celebrating the two year anniversary of getting my developer account. I started to contribute to KDE by sending minor patches and eventually in 2013 I participated in Season of KDE, the outreach program organized by KDE. Sebastian Kügler from the Plasma team mentored me. This was a great experience. After that I enrolled into Google Summer of Code twice as a student - this year I am helping to administrate Google Summer of Code and other mentoring programs for KDE. On the development side I currently work on Plasma Mobile, the free software eco-system for mobile devices.

Mentoring programs

The KDE Community runs and participates in various mentoring programs, for example Google Summer of Code, Google Code-in, Season of KDE and the FOSS Outreach Program for Woman. As I got into the KDE Community through one of this programs I am currently passing the torch and mentoring other students and helping to administrate these programs. One of the reason I feel good about this is that it gives me a feeling of "giving back". KDE as community welcomed me and made me one of them when I was eager to learn and contribute to the KDE Community. Now I am helping others experience the same. New contributors help to create a more diverse community and keeps the fun in the community intact. In my two years of experience with the KDE Community I've come across various new contributors from various professional and cultural backgrounds. This also helps the naive contributors to build their skills with help from existing contributors of KDE.

When I started contributing to KDE I didn't really have a lot of skills. All I knew was I wanted to contribute to KDE. At that time the Plasma team helped me to learn important aspects of programming and the KDE codebase. The first patch that I submitted had more then 20 issues to resolve. At that point I also learned an important skill: dealing with feedback effectively. Eventually I learned more skills and started to contribute to more advanced parts of the KDE Plasma Workspaces. For this I thank my mentors, Sebastian Kügler, Shantanu Tushar, Sinny Kumari, Marco Martin and the KDE Community as whole.

Plasma Mobile

The Plasma Mobile project's first prototype was revealed at Akademy 2015 by Sebastian Kügler and Boudewijn Rempt on behalf of the Plasma team. The Plasma Mobile project has the following vision:

> Plasma Mobile aims to become a complete software system for mobile devices. It is designed to give privacy-aware users back the full-control over their information and communication. Plasma Mobile takes a pragmatic approach and is inclusive to 3rd party software, allowing the user to choose which applications and services to use. It provides a seamless experience across multiple devices. Plasma Mobile implements open standards and it is developed in a transparent process that is open for the community to participate in.

Which in my opinion plays really well with the vision of KDE:

> A world in which everyone has control over their digital life and enjoys freedom and privacy.

From the start I was very excited about this project. Despite being a new project, the KDE Community already has experience working with non-desktop devices through the Plasma Active project. Currently I am working on building flashable images with Plasma Mobile. I believe Plasma Mobile is an important contribution to the Free Software movement, and I am glad to be a part of it.

I want to thank the whole KDE Community, every user, developer, artist, translator, ... You are the ones who makes it possible to dream of Konqi ruling the world. ;-)

23 The Motivation behind Contributing to KDE

Sanjiban Bairagya

Sanjiban Bairagya studied Information Technology at the National Institute of Technology, Durgapur, India. He currently works as a Software Engineer at Magicpin. He made his first contribution to KDE in 2013 and did a Google Summer of Code project with KDE's Marble team in 2014.

About 20 years ago, Matthias Ettrich proposed the creation of an easy-to-use desktop environment in which users could expect things to look, feel, and work consistently, something which was lacking in the Unix desktop at the time. This was the initial motivation that led to the birth of the KDE project, after a lot of people started showing interest in the idea. Initially the K in KDE was supposed to be termed as "Kool", but very soon it was decided that K should not stand for anything in particular, just call it "K Desktop Environment". I was introduced to KDE during my second year of college by some of my seniors around 4 years ago in 2012. That's when I installed Fedora with KDE, as my first Linux-based setup. At the time I looked at it as just a cool desktop having so many fun applications and widgets to use and play around with. In the beginning, I never gave a thought that I could be a part of building these applications. It was only towards the beginning of the following year that I thought of starting to contribute to its applications by coding. I used to use Marble, a virtual globe software, more than the others, so I started with that. At the time Marble had a pretty basic UI, with some new features just introduced that year, like the stars showing realistic colors and constellations, and draggable panels replacing the tab-based controls. The git reviewboard was the place to upload your patches at the time. And overall KDE was focused almost entirely on creating desktop applications. But more than the applications, its the welcoming community that encouraged me to keep continuing. The first time I had pinged Dennis, one of the main Marble developers, about contributing to Marble, in the #marble channel was in Jan 2013. If the conversation wouldn't have proceeded in such a welcoming way in which it did, I don't think I would have been encouraged to go any further. But that was just the beginning. And KDE has really evolved a lot since then.

KDE has gradually evolved itself from being a desktop environment, to now being part of almost every aspect of life that can be touched in terms of technology. The KDE Community has apps on Android now as well - KDE Connect and Marble Maps to name a few. KDE via Plasma Mobile even offers a free platform for mobile devices today, with a prototype already available. KDE Frameworks has come a long way, with its recent KF5 release. We even have a new place to upload our patches for review now, Phabricator, making it much easier to track their progress. Not only in terms of technology, the community has also become more diverse and vibrant now with more people contributing and participating in sprints and conferences from all across the globe. Not to mention, we have united our vision as well: "A world in which everyone has control over their digital life and enjoys freedom and privacy". And that is true indeed. It has been 4 years already that I have been using KDE software. Mostly because it undoubtedly does produce the best and most user-friendly products that free software has to offer. In fact, I grew so fond of it when I was in college, that we had even organized an event titled "Contributing to KDE" in the seminar room there, which was a grand success as well. And it did not stop there. Even now in the office, I installed Kubuntu on my laptop and after seeing me, some of my colleagues have switched to using Plasma and other KDE software as well. As a user and developer of KDE software, I feel it is my duty to spread the information as much as possible, and I have been doing just that. KDE gave me wings. The wings to know the world so much more, and be able to spend time in working with the most humble, knowledgeable, and welcoming people that can exist on planet Earth.

Now, looking at what the future of the KDE Community might turn out to be in a few more years from now, I think we should already acknowledge the fact that it is already the second largest Free Software community in the world right now (behind the Linux kernel community), and its numbers speaks for itself about the amount of freedom and friendliness that exists in the community. The rate at which KDE has progressed that I have seen in the last 3 years, there is no doubt but to know that there is no downhill from here. Having a conversation with the folks at KDE, you feel more closer to home than anywhere else, no matter which part of the world you come from. KDE has been among the leaders in desktop, and soon, with more people spending time on their phones than their desktops, it has entered the mobile platform as well. With the release of Plasma Mobile in full, people should be able to see a new world of KDE in the future as it keeps on developing. It's been 20 years since KDE was born, and if I imagine how it might be 20 years ahead from now, I can only see unparalleled progress. What could come next? Artificial Intelligence? Virtual Reality? Well, with its current rate of progress, along with its drive to fulfill its vision of everyone having control over their digital life, who knows, maybe it is evident that KDE will definitely keep spreading to the newest and latest technologies that will become a part of life for everyone in the future. As for us developers, what drives us to keep contributing is the very realization that our code touches so many lives and makes a difference. Coming back from a tiring day at the office, I think that contributing to free software you love to use is a very productive way to spend your free time. It can be any free software, I choose KDE because of its community of people with its free and open culture.

24 My Journey from Documentation to Continuous Integration

Scarlett Clark

Scarlett Clark has been an open source user since 1999 (Stacks of floppies!). Her first contributions began three years ago in KDE PIM documentation. She is now working on container packaging solutions, KDE continuous integration and a dash of Debian based packaging as time permits.

My journey started over three years ago with an email to the KDE documentation list asking a simple question, "How can I help?". Little did I know the adventures that would transpire from that email! I was quickly pointed to the KDE PIM team to assist them with some documentation. My first task was a massive rewrite of the KMail documentation, as it was very dated and in the worst shape. This progressed for some time, until I had to step down to resolve some health issues. Upon my return, I had briefly discussed with Valorie Zimmerman and Jonathan Riddell about helping out Kubuntu with some documentation as well. Thus begins a new adventure.

The next leg of my journey was Kubuntu. I was working on a bit of Wiki documentation, when Jonathan asked in IRC if anyone was interested in learning packaging. Me being the curious sort that I am, raised my virtual hand. This began a rather long journey into software packaging. It is an exciting facet of software, because you need to make everything work together and it is not always as straight forward as one would think. After some time of my packaging adventure, I was invited to my first Akademy! This was an amazing experience for someone rather new to Open Source contributions. It not only fueled me to further myself into contributing more, it got me closer to the people I have been working with online. It put faces to the IRC nicks! This I feel made a big difference in future online communications, as now personalities are known. Text does not really do justice to personalities and can be quite misunderstood. So now armed with a pile of new friends, I begin my next adventure into Season of KDE.

I had no knowledge of Season of KDE until Valorie had asked me if I would be interested in DevOps type work. She then linked the Season of KDE project to me, my thirst for knowledge triggered, thus beginning the next leg of my adventure. After getting approved for the project by Ben Cooksley (KDE's main sysadmin), I started on the revamp of build.kde.org. It began as quite a large learning curve, but as the pieces came together, it got easier. I successfully completed my Season of KDE project and launched my new build.kde.org automating job creation with groovy DSL. Seeing your creation go live for public consumption is an amazing feeling! With my packaging work and Season of KDE project, I was once again invited to Akademy. This Akademy was very special as I won an Akademy award[1]! The jury award to be exact, it was truly exciting to be recognized for all of the work I had put into the CI. The CI system is still a continuing work in progress. We have since moved to using docker containers for our builds. I have recently recruited some help to push forward the other platforms (Windows, Android, and OS X). With new knowledge and experience under my belt, I have rewritten the DSL once again to be much cleaner and extendable. So look forward to much more in the land of build.kde.org!

---

[1] award given out annually at Akademy to KDE contributors

25 A Place to Stay Forever

Sinny Kumari

Sinny Kumari joined the KDE family during late 2010. She worked mainly on Plasma Media Center and parts of Plasma. She loves talking about the KDE Community and its software. Other than that, she works toward motivating others to work on Open Source projects. In the daytime, she is a Software Engineer at Red Hat where she helps in maintaining Fedora and RHEL for PowerPC and s390x architectures.

It was late 2010 when I slowly started getting familiar with a new operating system called Linux which had the KDE Desktop environment with it. First, I started as a user and then slowly pushed myself to fix bugs. The first time I interacted with the community was by sending a patch for the File Watcher widget. As a beginner working on fixing the patch was not very easy. It required me to first download the source code and build Plasma and all required dependencies. Later, I had to find the right place where the fix should go and then re-compile the affected application and see whether the changes I made are working. Even though the changes I made were really small the experience I gained was not. It was an amazing feeling and experience to work with such a large community who develops loads of amazing software. I realized how different and fun it is to work on software which is used by millions of people compared to the way I was studying in college. This lead me to stick around the KDE Community even further.

My journey in KDE continued further as a volunteer for conf.kde.in 2011 in Bangalore, India. It was the first KDE conference happening in India and also the first KDE conference I attended. Thanks to Shantanu and Pradeepto who gave me a chance to be part of organizing it. It was fun to spread the news among colleges and explain to them why they should attend this conference. Lots of people came to attend it including college professors, working professionals but mainly students. I believe this conference opened the gates for a lot of students from India to contribute to KDE. For me, it was the first time I met people in-person from around the world and felt how awesome this community is. It increased my bond to KDE even further and felt like I am part of the KDE family.

With great enthusiasm, I planned to stay even longer here and contribute to KDE. As a result, I started getting into different KDE projects which interest me. I figured out that projects around Plasma (KDE's workspace) interest me more. Meanwhile, the Google Summer of Code period was also about to start, hence I applied to Plasma Media Center - the project that has always stayed close to my heart. Plasma Media center is a KDE application which aims to provide an easy media experience (music, pictures, videos) to people on a device running KDE Plasma. It supports browsing and viewing media local to your system as well as available from online services like YouTube, Flickr etc. Many thanks to Marco Martin who mentored me to get this project in good shape. While writing this, I recall how different family members from KDE participated to shape this project even better and helped it to mature - in terms of code, design, spreading the news, packaging, motivating and so on. I remember writing blog posts and articles for KDE's official news site about Plasma Media Center releases and how happy people were to see it growing from desktop to tablets and extending to TV. KDE love is always about spreading it to more people. Later on in KDE India conferences and meetups, we used to talk about and give demos of Plasma Media Center to attendees. We explained how to create an awesome UI application like Plasma Media Center using Qt/KDE. Attendees used to love this application and liked to contribute to it. As a result, we were able to pull in even more people to work and continue evolving Plasma Media Center further along to a long journey. With continuous effort of loads of people, Plasma Media Center's codebase matured from Playground (the place where new KDE software starts its life) to Extragear (where mature software lives that is not part of the main release cycle), and then to the main release cycle. The journey of this project's success was not easy but not impossible either. It reached this maturity level only because of love from different people in the KDE Community. Sadly, these days due to job and other responsibilities I don't have time to work on it. But I am positive that it will keep getting love in the future from my other KDE family members.

Life keeps moving on further and so does love towards the KDE Community and its software. In order to maintain, improve and have new software in KDE, it is important that together we keep on expanding our family while keeping everyone involved. This friendly and loving nature of community members will always keep new/existing contributors feel welcomed and homely while working on KDE projects.

26 A Learning Paradise

David Narváez

David Narváez is a PhD student in Computer Science at RIT in Rochester, NY, USA. Originally from Panama, he is the current maintainer of Kig, an application for interactive geometry that is part of the KDE Education Project.

I joined the KDE Community back in 2009 to fix a couple of bugs and never left. I was one to scratch my own itch in any application I would use frequently: from Kig, which was my main interest, to KDevelop which I used to work on Kig, to Plasma because I was using it to manage my desktop environment. KDE was certainly not the only FOSS community I contributed code to, but no other community was as enticing as KDE. At the beginning, I could not really point the finger at what the reason for this was.

At the same time I was learning the trade as a professional software engineer (which, in my culture is nothing but a name for a glorified computer programmer) back in Panama, my home country. At the peak of my contributions to KDE, I had a full time job as a software engineer, coding several hours a day, only to come home and code several more hours working on KDE-related stuff. Many would say I spent my entire day coding, but for me these were two completely different activities.

I eventually realized that the differentiating factor was learning. KDE was much more than a developer community for me: it was a learning environment. My daytime job, on the other hand, did not foster innovation and learning. This was not a problem particular to my employer at the time, but a more general issue about the culture among software developers in my home country. While I understand not everybody is as excited about learning as I am, I can objectively argue that KDE, as a learning community, prepared me better for a global market and gave me a better chance at several other opportunities that came by later in life. Here I describe some of the core values I found in KDE that I could not have found inside the software developer market in my home country:

- In KDE we have a horizontal structure promoting code review, open design discussions, collaborative coding, etc. In contrast, my daytime job at the time had a vertical structure where fixing bugs in somebody else's code was considered an offense, and trying new technologies was never an option during design discussions.

- Proposing the adoption of new ideas and paradigms in my workplace would almost always meet the mantra of "we have always done it this way". In contrast, I joined the KDE Community as a developer just a couple of years after KDE adopted a whole new approach to desktop environments through KDE 4.

- KDE is, by definition, a global community. As such, you will always deal with not only different time zones, but also different cultures. I vividly remember waking up at five in the morning to read code reviews from people at 7 time zones away, and improve my code based on their feedback before leaving for my paid work. Right around those years, the software development market in my home country was starting to globalize, and as a consequence, people started thinking about different time zones. When it was my turn to deal with these issues, it felt like home because of my KDE experience.

- From the merely technical point of view, the various software architectures used across KDE projects made it possible for me to explore paradigms and designs that were not popular inside the market in Panama. My exposure to these ideas turned some of the more challenging tasks of my day job into straightforward adaptations of problems that had already been solved inside the KDE Community.

I am convinced it is because of all these values we have forged as a community inside KDE that I was able to pursue many opportunities that would have been way out of my reach had I been equipped only with the knowledge I could acquire in the local market. But Panama is not the only country in the world where the digital divide is keeping developers with great potential from acquiring all the knowledge they need to be competitive in the global market. In fact, most of the skills and experience that are highly valued in the IT market (think of fluent English, or early exposure to computers) are native to a small fraction of the planet which we usually refer to as the first world. In the age of information, communities like KDE play the role of forges of global talent that will enable important changes in our digital lives. And although my personal journey in KDE has improved my IT skills, the global talent we attract as a community does not necessarily need to be programmers: some of our most active contributors work on designs, translations, technical writing and even marketing; all of which are areas with their own global markets and needs. What is in it for all of us, is that our participation in the community also brings along experiences that are stepping stones in our paths to achieve personal goals.

Today, I have moved away from the industry and into research, doing doctoral studies. This move has meant leaving my home country, adapting to new places and having less time to contribute code to Free Software in general. Yet, KDE is still an important part of what I do and, as such, I care about its future. Since I consider the KDE Community an enabler of opportunities, I see our products as means to a greater goal that is helping the world through innovation. This point of view is what drives me every time I contribute to KDE, because it is as exciting to think about where I can take KDE as it is to think about where KDE can take us. Thus, it is my first and foremost priority, looking into the future, to preserve this nature of our community. I believe this, and not the technology we produce, is the key to staying relevant for the next 20 years. In this context, outreach and mentoring naturally translates to more opportunities as more people get involved, and I cannot think of a better excuse to strive for world domination :)

27 The Circle of Four Steps to Become a Good Developer

Sune Vuorela

Sune Vuorela is a software developer who has been around KDE and other open source projects for more than a decade. Sune works as a software consultant doing Qt and C++ and whatever else is needed, mostly in areas of logistics or medical technologies. When not in front of a computer, Sune enjoys cooking, reading books, and being outdoors. Either alone, or with the scouts.

KDE recently formulated a vision:

> A world in which everyone has control over their digital life and enjoys freedom and privacy.

Free software is a important step for that vision, and that has been how KDE has done its things since forever. But for free software to matter, people also need to be able to take advantage of the freedom they are given. Having more and better developers is needed for that. Partially to be able to understand code, partially to be able to write readable code. Both plays into being a good developer, and especially for newcomers asking how to become a good developer is a frequent question.

When I have the time and am in a joyful mood, my answer has been "Just follow Sune's four steps", partly serious, partly tongue in cheek, because they aren't actually formally described anywhere.

This is an attempt to write it up and how they are applied within various KDE projects as a part of KDE producing many new skilled developers.

The four circular steps to become a good developer are:

- Read some theory
- Write some code
- Read other people's code
- Have other people read your code

These steps can be applied in any order, but to become a good developer it is important to visit all steps frequently.

Read some theory

Extending your base of knowledge is an important thing to always be doing. Depending on your area of expertise and interests, it can be anything from reading about what a for-loop is, to the newest upcoming meta programming features in the upcoming standard of C++, the theory behind the Java Virtual Machine or how to do basic OpenGL for games. A simple, but important theory document originating from KDE is the document about binary compatibility in C++ libraries[1].

The theory can just be an introduction to new design patterns or a starter guide in a new programming language. But read. Learn. Try. Which leads me straight to the next point about writing code.

Write some code

No one ever becomes a good developer without practical coding experience, or as they says it at the scouts, "Learning by Doing". Not all code should be production quality or actually meet the public eye, but do publish as much as possible. It helps you and others with many of the other steps. Write code for fun. For experimentation. And for actual real life use cases. Have experimentation projects

---

[1] https://community.kde.org/Policies/Binary_Compatibility_Issues_With_C++

both in your primary programming languages as well as other programming languages. Maybe the other programming languages have features you like that are coming soon to your primary programming languages. This points nicely back to reading some theory.

KDE offers a quite fast "code to production" path with a large userbase that helps keep up the motivation for actually writing code. In order to be able to write better code, getting experience with other people's code and improving other people's code is a really good way to become a better developer. And this points again forward to the next point about reading code.

Read other people's code

A part of being able to know what good code is is to see good code, as well as bad code. Especially in various open source projects, it is very easy to get a hold of other people's code.

Reading other people's code leads directly to writing better code, as well as pointing to interesting areas for studying more theory.

The code reading can both be in private behind closed doors, or as part of public/formal code reviews, where you can discuss the code and suggest improvements.

By reading other people's code, one learns a lot by example about what to do and what not to do, and usually it ends up supporting the theory one has read. A simple thing like the importance of proper variable and function naming becomes much more clear once one has tried reading both code where the original author(s) had cared for that kind of details, and reading code where all variable names are single letter ones. Once you have tried reading both, you know how it actually helps.

KDE has only open source code, so it is easily available for anyone to learn from, and several KDE projects also have optional or mandatory code reviews for all new code, where everyone can jump in and participate in the code review to let both the reviewer and the author learn from each other.

Have other people read your code

You need to know when you have done well and where you have room for improvements. When contributing to existing projects, the current developers usually review your code and help you raise the quality if needed.

KDE is full of people who do what they do for fun, and put a lot of work into ensuring that whatever code they have is maintainable. Reviewing incoming code is important for this. This also gives a unique opportunity to discuss your possible code changes with the original authors of whatever piece of code you are contributing to.

KDE has several systems in place for that. New projects have to go through an initial review to ensure that the basics are sane, and many subprojects either have optional or mandatory code review where experienced developers have to sign off on new code for existing projects.

End notes

These four steps are crucial to continuously educate both new and existing developers. Most people want to get better at what they like doing, and this approach really helps. There is no requirement to spend an equal amount of time and energy on all steps, but all steps should be revisited. Also, make sure to occasionally get out of your comfort zone to learn something new.

Interacting with others around your code is important, and working with an existing code base is often better to learn from, in both good and bad ways, than starting all projects from scratch. KDE with its 20 years of history has an amazing code base and an amazing set of experienced and new people always helping each other in making everyone better.

28 How We Make Plasma

Sebastian Kügler

Sebastian Kügler is a core developer at KDE and Free Software activist. Being involved in the creation of the Plasma desktop from the beginning, Sebastian lead the development of its recent version, Plasma 5 as part of his job as Chief of Operations at Blue Systems. Sebastian has been release manager throughout the KDE 4 series and initiated KDE's Marketing Working Group. He was part of the KDE e.V.'s Board of Directors from 2006 to 2013. On the technical side, sebas' develops and maintains several of KDE Plasma's key components.

The KDE project originated from the wish to create a consistent workspace environment that made Linux devices accessible to normal users by offering a graphical interface. Since its inception, 20 years ago, the KDE Desktop, nowadays called "Plasma" surpassed this initial goal and today offers one of the most popular workspace user interfaces. In many aspects, it represents the state of the art of computing.

In this article, we are going to have a closer look at various aspects of Plasma, its evolution, how it is used and developed, and why it exists in the first place.

The User Story

A desktop is the primary user interface of a computer, it allows to start apps, switch between windows and offers access to configure system-level functions, such as hardware support and the general behavior of the desktop and software. 20 years ago, KDE was the first of its kind, X11 was still pretty young, and consistency a concept almost unheard of on Linux systems. Developers looked at competitors like SUN Microsystem's CDE, and wanted to offer a modern replacement as Freedom software.

KDE 1 released relatively quickly, given the gargantuan task, and laid the base for many further development. Looking through the code-base, we still often encounter code written 20 years back. Today, millions of users around the world rely on Plasma on a daily basis. It is the tool that makes their computer useful. While many users do not particularly care (and that's a good thing: Plasma should be a tool that helps you to get the job done), there is also a large number of people who deeply care, who follow every change developers make and who install new versions with excitement and anticipation.

To many users, Plasma enables them to do what they want, how they want. Plasma's flexibility and configurability is unparalleled, even in proprietary software. Users demand to be met with respect, and do not want to be limited, but rather enabled by the software they use.

Plasma has become a professional tool, today it is used in large enterprises, schools, governmental organizations at different levels. Not long ago, it was even spotted in the control room of the Large Hadron Collider, the biggest and most complex machine in the world.

Development model

Plasma is developed at a rapid pace. 4 yearly feature releases are followed up by a number of stabilization and translation updates. Plasma is developed in a collaborative fashion, based on consensus. There is no single person that decides about features and priorities, but rather a team of maintainers that take decision based on user feedback, consensus and the available resources. Mailing lists, IRC chats and weekly video conferences keep communication channels tight and make sure that problems can be addressed in a timely manner.

This quick succession of releases and cycles is made possible by a huge amount of technology in the background. Every change a developer commits leads to automated builds in different configurations and unit-testing. Feedback about mistakes in the code is automated to ensure a higher quality and less interruption in operation and development. Users who want to follow development closely and help testing can nowadays even get their fix daily in the form of daily updated packages directly from Plasma's git master. Continuous building and integration makes rapid development possible. Modern tools like git and Phabricator foster developer collaboration, and there is a strong culture of code reviews in the Plasma team.

Quality has become a central part of the goal of Plasma's development model. A code-base as complex as Plasma and its underlying stack is hard to "get right". Quality problems usually stem from a relatively complex task to solve: users will run Plasma on random hardware, drivers vary in quality. Plasma sits on top of a modular, but complex software stack that is also moving rapidly. It is not always easy to catch up with changes in underlying systems, such as Qt, D-Bus, the graphics stack, the Linux kernel and its close relatives.

Methods and Tools

The Plasma team has adopted several modern software engineering practices. Back in the days, the user interface of the KDE Desktop was often designed by the same people who wrote the software. It often simply reflected what the code could do. Nowadays, a team of designers has a say in almost every user-visible change, and larger changes are carefully planned in advance keeping in mind how it solves the user's problem and how it fits into the whole of the software environment. On the software development side, test-driven development is making inroads into KDE's and Plasma's development processes. While it is not possible to automatically test every single function call and behavioral expectation, more and more code is covered by a battery of tests that are run regularly. This avoids unintended breakage and speeds up the development by reducing the need for tedious, time-consuming manual testing.

Both, product and project decisions are being taken by the core team of developers, in consensus with a group of designers, other developers and based on user needs. Product-level decisions are more and more influenced by product-level thinking, although this is a process which is only being adopted within the past years. Development happens openly, the central discussion forum is the plasma-devel mailing list. A new project management tool has been adopted in 2015, the Plasma team now uses Phabricator, a web-based collaboration platform to structure tasks, review code and discuss changes in general. Phabricator's git integration presents a clear and logical workflow to get changes developed, reviewed and merged. Issue tracking is done in KDE's Bugzilla instance. Most developers have a love and hate relationship to Bugzilla, as it can feel a bit like handling a monster. Practically, however, Bugzilla's usefulness is pretty much unparalleled. It is a proven tool for software quality assurance that has lead to many users receiving fixes for their problem. bugs.kde.org provides a powerful and well-used feedback mechanism, and forms an essential part of the development process.

In the past, KDE software was built by engineers, for engineers and user interface design was not always a strong point. Now, user experience experts and interaction designers have become important contributors all over Plasma. Instead of a top-down approach on design and functionality, the user experience experts are embedded in the development process at a deeper level. The development of Plasma 5 has seen an increased focus also on visual quality, it has refined and redefined its design language, without sacrificing flexibility, functionality or negatively impacting technical architecture.

Nowadays, technical quality, visual coherence and smooth interaction design have become equally important. Plasma does not baby, but empower the user to get the work done.

The Technology Story

Frameworks, QtQuick and Plasma 5

In its first three iterations, kdelibs, a monolithic library on top of Qt which shared functionality and code across KDE applications and the desktop. In its first iterations, KDE was technically a more or less monolithic thing. While it was very powerful from the get-go, it grew organically and eventually became a big and interdependent platform on top of Qt. Your editor remembers discussions about the scalability limits with this approach already back in 2005. KDE 4 took the first step into a more modular world by coarsely splitting kdelibs into topical libraries. Internally, there were rather big sections of entangled functionality, however. These were finely split up in the development cycle of the fifth iteration of "kdelibs", and first released separately as a consistent set of modules offering more than 50 individual frameworks with a clearly defined dependency structure and backwards compatible future releases in quick cycles with tight quality control. Frameworks 5 has worked out very well from a technology point of view and covers a very wide range of needs. Thanks to its modular structure it allows the creation of leaner apps that are smaller in footprint, easier to deploy and load faster.

Devices

In the Plasma 4 cycle, we have seen the first user interface built for non-desktop devices. An experimental phone UI built with Plasma technology successfully held a phone call as early as 2010. Plasma 5 has been designed for deployment on different devices. Plasma today will on most machines load a desktop UI module and components suitable for use with a mouse, touchpad and keyboard. Indeed, the highest priority for Plasma's fifth iteration was to build up the desktop that is functionally equivalent with previous releases, using Frameworks 5. In the same release, the move to QtQuick for the user interface components of the workspace has been completed.

This architecture allows sharing components across devices at multiple levels, and a high degree of code-reuse. It allows to improve the user experience across devices, and in combination a consistent-to-use cross-device experience. The Plasma Phone project, for example, shares roughly 90% of the code with the desktop, without sacrificing usability. Reversely, Plasma technology allows to develop applications that work not just on one device, but across a range of devices, adapting its user interface to the hardware used.

Graphics and Wayland

Looking down the graphics stack, we have finally reached a point where we usually render the entire user interface using hardware acceleration on the graphics card. Smoother graphical effects, better energy efficiency and more CPU resources being available to the applications all make for rather user-visible improvements. Not all is rosy in the graphics world however, and driver problems hurt many users. At the same time, KDE's user base enjoys an incredible variety in hardware and setups. Some run it on a small laptops, others on powerful multi-core machines connected to a video wall – all expect Plasma to handle the job gracefully. Aside from the workspace, a component that has seen serious modernization over the past years is Kwin, Plasma's window manager and compositor. Pluggable hardware and rendering backends, exchangeable user interface elements such as task switchers make Kwin a very versatile window manager. Over the past years, Kwin has gained support for running as a Wayland compositor. It now provides both modes, running on top of an X11 server or starting its own Wayland compositor that provides the graphics rendering and input for applications. A Wayland session uses a much leaner graphics stack, protocols which guarantee pixel perfection by using more modern and more clearly defined semantics. Kwin's Wayland mode is in fact already used in Plasma Mobile's phone user interface, and is being readied for desktop end users this year.

Developing and maintaining a codebase such as Plasma's is not an easy job, but having the architectural work on modularization behind us, these areas will improve over time as we get more and more fixes into our codebase, upstream and downstream.

Roadmap Story

For the next years, there are no major architectural changes planned for Plasma – other than making Plasma available on Wayland. This means that the focus shifts more to user-visible changes, bugfixing, polishing and performance improvements. Additional features can be added without affecting the core thanks to Plasma's modular structure.

Developers want to make Plasma a serious contender for professional use-cases. This means that stability and quality shifts into focus. Indeed, the primary focus of the current development cycle is bugfixing and quality improvements.

In devices-land, Plasma has yet to make inroads. Developers continue to improve the mobile shell and related technology. In the long-run, Plasma could stick to the desktop, which is becoming more and more of a niche market, so it will lead to less relevance overall. The strategy to make Plasma as a technology and as a workspace available also on non-desktop devices will at some point prove essential to the survival of Plasma. Already today, the mobile efforts supplement the desktop by improving performance, footprint and give the codebase much wider testing.

Your editor once said himself: "I want Plasma to help me get my work done so I can go diving": Plasma is not a purpose in itself, but a tool that allows using other tools (your computer, applications) efficiently. It should get out of the way as much as possible, but when needed it should be there and have the right tools available at your fingertips. It should do all this gracefully and elegantly, and give a feel of quality and that I am really using the best tool for this job. Users come for the features and the look, and they stay for the freedom and privacy aspects. Plasma shows excellence in both areas.

29 Evolution of Windowing Systems

Martin Gräßlin

Martin Gräßlin is a KDE developer since 2008 with the primary focus on KWin, the window manager and compositor of the KDE Plasma workspaces. He is employed by BlueSystems GmbH to work on KWin and Plasma.

When Matthias Ettrich announced the Kool Desktop Environment it was intended for Linux/Unix and by that also for the X11 Windowing System. At that time it was the only available windowing system for Unix-like systems. Matthias didn't want to write a dedicated window manager for this system. He thought that "at the beginning, the KDE panel will work as an Fvwm-Module".

Nowadays KWin, the window manager started by Matthias for KDE 2 in 1999, is one of the oldest components in the KDE Plasma workspaces and the largest single code base of Plasma. It is one of the pillars of Plasma and an extremely important part of the user experience of Plasma. KWin, unlike many other components from KDE 2, survived several technology transitions. The biggest threat to the existence of KWin was the time before KDE 4 was released. A disruption on the desktop happened: Compiz! Finally there was the chance to unify the desktop world and have just one major window manager.

Compiz was a huge change. It made use of "compositing" directly in the window manager. Compositing is a kind of hack added to the X windowing system to make it possible to have translucent windows. The extensions allow interested applications to get notified when a window changes its content (damage extension) and to redirect the windows from rendering directly to the X-Server to a pixmap (composite extension). A compositor can now take all the windows pixmaps and render them as the final image, making use of translucency, arranging them in different ways and applying smooth transitions. One of the core parts of the XServer got replaced by two extensions and an additional application. It was a sign of defeat in retrospection. The X developers decided to hand over responsibility to other applications because the XServer was not able to deliver the required features.

In the beginning there was only xcompmgr and various forks (including one by KDE) - an additional process adding translucency, drop shadows and simple animations, not integrated in any way with the window manager. Compiz changed that significantly. A window manager built around the idea of compositing, making use of OpenGL for all rendering. It demonstrated functionality which just was not possible on other systems. Of course KDE wanted to integrate that technology and Compiz was a true competitor to KWin. Yours truly, a user back at that time, questioned the sanity of the KDE developers to implement compositing in KWin instead of just using Compiz. The problem for Compiz back then at the end of the first decade of this century was the hard dependency on compositing and on OpenGL. Both are things which could not be guaranteed. Basing your environment on this technology was not an option (yet) and having two window manager with different sets of functionality was not a good idea. So the better option was to extend the excellent window manager KWin with the functionality of a compositor: KWin 4 was born.

But over the years we learned how much compositing was more of a hack than a proper solution. Why is it not possible to have thumbnails for minimized windows? Yes one can hack around this as well, but then legacy applications might think they are not minimized and continue to play the video instead of pausing it and more. Why does it have to stutter when unminimizing a window? Why is it not possible to transform the pointer input events in a way that it matches the transformed window positions? Why do we get invalid screen content when a window first opens (especially when using

OpenGL)? Why is it not possible to resize windows in truly smooth ways?

And then there is the problem of security. X11 being designed in the 1980s completely lacks the idea of malicious processes. It is trivial to write a key logger, it is super easy to get to the content of the windows and their positions. This allows all kinds of wonderful attacks. Your malicious application wants to get the user's password: just replace the lock screen. Your malicious application wants to get the root password: just install a key logger when a window asking for the password is added. You want to take over the browser and send it to fakebank.com instead of bank.com: just send the right key events and put a window on top of the browser to simulate that you are on bank.com.

This all shows that X11 is not suited for today's world - neither for desktop nor for mobile. Something new was needed, something like an X12. Many contenders existed to replace the aging X windowing system, but none gained traction. Except for Wayland. A new windowing system, designed from ground up with the aim of "every frame perfect". Designed by X11 developers applying the lessons learned from X and taking the good things to the new world.

This development again means a disruption for Plasma and especially KWin. A system based around X11, developed for X11. How should that ever go to Wayland. Maybe it is easier to write a new system from scratch? Something which gets rid of the legacy and does it right from the start? But what if Wayland fails just like all the other X-replacement-systems? The community decided to go the long walk: bring the system to the new world without having to rewrite everything. Especially for KWin this meant a huge effort. The code base needed to become windowing system independent, needed to support both X11 and Wayland windows.

Now this effort is slowly reaching an end. This article is written in a Plasma session on Wayland in a KWrite using Wayland instead of X11. But of course it will still be a long way till we finally get rid of X11. There are many X11 specific functionalities which are essential to users' workflows, but which are built around the insecure parts of

X11. It will take time to identify the workflows and add sufficient (and secure) replacements.

30 Twenty Years of Email

Volker Krause

Volker Krause joined KDE in 2002, and primarily contributed to KDE's email and personal information management infrastructure and applications. He works as a software engineer, consultant and trainer at KDAB.

On October 14, 1996 Matthias Ettrich started KDE, with an RFC822 message, the same message format still in use today two decades later, with just minor fixes and extensions for supporting non-ASCII text. We all know this as email.

Shortly after, still in 1996, KDE's own email client, KMail, was started. While it mutated heavily several times in its almost twenty years of history, you can still find traces of its founders in the code today.

Email has always been an essential component of KDE, although a lot has changed, and will continue to change. It is interesting to look at the developments and challenges in this way, as these are also reflected in many other areas of KDE, and beyond.

Enabling Access

Back when KMail was started, the prevalent way of using email was downloading and storing it locally on a single personal computer, with ISPs or universities providing POP3 accounts that buffered incoming emails until the user had a chance to fetch them. With email becoming popular and important on a larger scale, various companies tried to push their proprietary variants, such as Lotus Notes and Microsoft Exchange.

Therefore the first challenge was to provide free access to email, both free of cost and with the freedoms guaranteed by Free Software. This might seem odd from a present point of view, where we are used to finding Free Software applications for pretty much any use case.

In the first years of KDE, Free Software as such was not yet universally accepted. On the contrary, it had to face massive opposition, in particular from Microsoft. It took years to prove that Free Software was a development model that could provide high quality and innovative applications, something that is hardly questioned anymore by now. Even Microsoft is contributing actively to Free Software today.

KMail, together with many many other Free Software applications, proved the opponents of the GPL wrong, having become a competitive product, with some of its innovations such as the missing attachment warning having found their way into many other email clients. And it has found a balance between purism regarding open standards and pragmatism when it comes to compatibility with proprietary applications, still an ongoing discussion in the Free Software world.

In order to enable free access to your data, free applications are essential. As the world changes however, this is challenged over and over again, and free applications are not the only piece in the puzzle any more.

Clouds

As computing equipment, and email with it, became more and more ubiquitous, a new challenge arose at the beginning of the century. With the availability of laptops, and later smartphones, email needed to be available on multiple devices simultaneously; the old download model did not work anymore.

With the widespread availability of permanent internet connectivity in the wake of the dot-com boom, the solution turned out to be server-side storage and online access, an approach that years later became associated with the term "cloud".

IMAP, the protocol for server-side email storage and access was standardized, and KMail received support for it. While solving the problem in theory, the limited availability of email providers offering affordable IMAP hosting at the time did not really help though.

Instead, advertisement-based webmail providers started to appear and became popular, offering cost-free email hosting with access from a browser, and a few megabytes of storage space. That entire market got swept away with the appearance of Gmail in 2004 though, which offered an (at the time) audacious one gigabyte of storage space, and a stream of innovations in the user interface. Gmail has since become the de-facto standard for consumer email.

The implications of this were not immediately recognized by everyone, and the inside perspective tends to be skewed. We understand the risks and implications of the cloud approach ("there is no cloud, just other people's computers"), and we have access to alternatives, but that is not what the average user sees when looking at Gmail. It is a solution to a very real and pressing problem, and even seemingly free of cost.

KMail, of course, has dedicated support for Gmail and its various non-standard extensions nowadays. But regarding having control over your own data, is that really the way we envision our communication infrastructure?

How and where data is stored and how it is accessed have become just as important as having a free application to access it, and this is more than providing a Free Software server implementation. We also need to offer solutions for secure and reliable hosting and deployment. "Just run your own email infrastructure" is not a viable solution for most users. Finding convincing and practical answers to this will be an important challenge for the Free Software community in the coming years, KDE included.

Small Screens

In 2007 the iPhone started the age of the smartphone. A year later, Android followed. By 2012 a billion devices had been sold, making a small touch screen with barely more than a ten centimeter diagonal the world's primary communication interface.

First attempts to give KMail a smartphone-compatible interface happened in 2010, with limited success. The way we organize and use email is inherently tree-based. Folders, message threads and in-line conversations can all get deeply nested. Tree-based interfaces however only work poorly on small screens, either being very cumbersome to use or imposing severe restrictions on the nesting depth.

Not only KMail was affected by this challenge though. This situation contributed to the rise of a new style of communication approach: messenger apps. By linearizing conversations, they avoid the user interface challenges email poses on small screens, quickly gaining hundreds of millions of users.

Unlike email however, the messengers, no matter if using proprietary or open source clients, are not using standardized and interoperable protocols, turning them into communication islands relying on vendor-hosted server infrastructure.

Gmail and proprietary messengers are challenging conventional email clients, in particular in the consumer space. Even heavyweights like Thunderbird struggle with this. Solutions that allow you to regain control over your communication data, without losing the convenience and functionality proprietary solutions provide right now, have yet to be found.

Silos

The smartphone platforms also made application bundles a widely-used technology, to support their application stores and increase security on the devices. Application bundles since then have also become relevant on all other major platforms.

Isolation from broken or malicious applications and straightforward deployment and cleanup make application bundles a very attractive choice.

On the other hand, application bundles lead to the creation of silos. Data and functionality is only available to a single application, and the rest of the workspace cannot benefit from it.

Because the KDE community acts as both application vendor and a platform vendor in this model, the KMail team is faced with a dilemma. In order to be easy to deploy on the most widely-used platforms (Windows, Android) an application architecture that allows the creation of an application bundle would be needed. On the Plasma workspace however, deep integration would be desirable, providing access to email communication for the entire platform.

KMail has chosen to go "all in" on the platform integration side, with a multi-process architecture enabling data sharing and non-exclusive data access. This is a prerequisite to offering a free and privacy-honoring answer to the personal digital assistants for example.

Other KDE applications are focusing on application bundle compatibility instead. There is no right or wrong here, but finding a way to serve both scenarios will be a major technical challenge for many KDE libraries and applications going forward.

Privacy and Freedom

Providing secure communication can be traced back to the early days of KMail. Support for PGP encryption was added in November 1997, and support for transport encryption followed soon after. Growing interest in security, also in the form of public funding, resulted in the joint Gpg4Win project together with the GnuPG community, with KDE providing the Kleopatra certificate manager.

In May 2013 Edward Snowden gave the world a glimpse of the extent of global mass surveillance. What were once considered paranoid speculations suddenly looked naive, and unless you took measures to protect your privacy, privacy itself turned out to be only an illusion.

Not only is all your communication intercepted and recorded, it is also automatically analyzed by machine learning algorithms that decide what is "normal" and what is suspicious. You lose your freedom to be different, and uncontrollable machines decide the consequences of that. It has become very apparent that privacy is an essential prerequisite for freedom.

Free Software is well positioned to ensure privacy when it comes to your digital footprints. Free Software is probably the only way to ensure that. And without conflicting commercial interest in KDE getting in the way, our users are not our product, and we can truly follow the "privacy by default" maxim.

As news about the extent of the mass surveillance spread, demand for Gpg4Win tripled, with monthly downloads crossing the 100,000 mark. KMail also saw a renewed interest in improving encryption features, in particular by making them easier to use. "Privacy by default" also means the software needs to do everything it can to ensure privacy if the user does not understand the intricate details of public key encryption and certificate trust chains.

Today KDE technology is helping millions of users to protect the integrity and privacy of their email content. There is still more to do though. Content encryption is only addressing part of the issue, and protecting metadata of email communication is an equally important and still unsolved problem.

Conclusion

Matthias got what he had asked for, and so much more. What KDE in particular and Free Software in general achieved in the last two decades is beyond what would have been imaginable in 1996.

People have questioned the relevance of the desktop, the relevance of email or that of KMail in today's world. All this of course might or might not change in the future. That is not the most important question going forward though. It is who will have control over your data. And that is not just affecting email. What is the point of Calligra if your documents are locked in a proprietary Google or Microsoft cloud? What is the point of our scientific and educational software if you cannot afford the corresponding textbooks? What is the point of our communication software if the world uses proprietary messengers?

Obviously free applications will stay a key element for this, but we also need to look at the bigger picture and continuously reevaluate if we still provide a valid solution to whatever the original problem has evolved into by now. With ubiquitous connectivity and software so deeply embedded into every aspect of our lives, we cannot look at applications on their own anymore. We need to look for solutions for today and tomorrow's use cases that allow you to retain and regain control of your data, striving for a world in which everyone has control over their digital life and enjoys freedom and privacy.

31 Krita Animation

Timothée Giet

Timothée Giet is a graphic artist from France, using exclusively free software since 2010. He works mainly on free software or freely licensed projects, doing all kinds of graphical work from illustration to icon design, and also teaching and creating training materials. He is a regular contributor to Krita and GCompris.

Let me tell you the story about Krita and animation. For me, it started in 2010 when I discovered Krita. I was impressed by the quality of its drawing tools, and since I was looking for a free software alternative that would allow me to draw comics and animations, I secretly wished you could draw animations with it.

Imagine how excited I was when, just the next year, a new mysterious contributor actually started working on an external plugin to add some animation tools. It was not easy to use nor very stable, but it was a good sign that other people wanted this.

Around the same time, thanks to KDE e.V., I could attend the Libre Graphics Meeting where I met for the first time Boudewijn, the maintainer of Krita. During our conversation, I told him how great it would be if we could add some internal animation tools. It sounded a bit crazy at the time, and we both agreed that lot of work was needed first to get a solid drawing software, but the idea was there.

This first animation plugin experiments did not progress very much, and the main author left them unfinished. Later in 2013, a more serious project started with a Google Summer of Code student trying to add some internal animation tools. Sadly, even after two years, the plugin still was not production-ready and did not progress much. The contributions were still in a separate branch and not yet integrated in the main binary.

It was finally in 2015 that another Google Summer of Code student managed to really integrate the animation tools, learning from the mistakes in previous attempts. Now we have Krita 3.0, officially released and including basic animation tools. Animators from all over the world quickly started adopting it and sent some positive feedback.

But this is only the beginning. We are still working on adding more tools and features, and I have no doubt that Krita will soon become a famous software tool in the animation world, if it hasn't already. It is a big step forward for people creating multimedia content exclusively with free software (for the operating system as for the tools). We now have a quite complete ecosystem of tools available in which Krita provides a missing piece for traditional animators. Let's see what people will create with it.

32 The Transient Nature of Design

Nuno Pinheiro

Nuno Pinheiro is a Portuguese graphic designer and illustrator. He specializes in iconography, themes and user interface design. Nuno's works include general illustrations, UI design, web design, corporate design as well as other works in creative areas. Known for his work in the Oxygen Project where he is the current coordinator of a design platform with 2000+ icons, wallpapers, sound effects and window styles. His computer art is used on KDE computer platforms worldwide. Over the last years he engaged in coding with QML creating fine tuned experiences for users and became interested in the Developer/Designer Interface. He works as a UX/UI designer, consultant and trainer at KDAB.

The Tempos of Oxygen

Design in open source is special. At least to me it is, and has always been, and the reason for that is simple: the relative ephemerality of it, so unlike other open source projects where the beginning is well defined but the end is something to be avoided. In design and especially in this post-modern ever-recursive design landscape the end is as present as its beginning, and so it must be fully embraced.

So... What is the point of it? I mean if it is done to have an end what does it achieve? This creates a problem that I'm sure every design related open source project has debated with itself.

For Oxygen and me personally it was solved with the assumption of three time periods: a future, present and past. That looking back has now been reverted.

Its Past was its Future

So what drove me to design and open source? I guess this is where, for me, design shares more with common "traditional open source projects": an itch to scratch, or more specifically a couple of emoticons in an instant messaging app I used in my favorite desktop at the time (KDE 3.X). So I made a couple of icons (really low quality) but was encouraged by the wonderful community to keep working on it and so I did. And as a result of my continued engagement with the community, I was invited to be a part of this new project – Oxygen. In its infancy it was a Future, it was everything, and anything, the solution to all problems. It was also a repository of all my uncertainties and doubts (all founded, I might add), but it was a fantastic time, a time to get to know what you are and how you express it, a time to realize that working within a group of people is far more challenging but also far more rewarding than all by yourself. A time to make mistakes, a time to correct those mistakes and a time to realize the extension of your errors would mean, you would need to start all over. In the end what comes out is Oxygen, a child of its time, a son of Everaldo Coelho, Crystal Icon set of Nuvola by dear friend and Oxygen colleague David Vignoni. It was an icon set and it was amazing. The future offspring of some superb parents - and trust me we stood on the shoulders of giants - for its time Oxygen's parents were, in many ways, ground breaking feats of computer design not just in open source but in computer design, rivaling with the best of the best in the industry.

This realization made me become fully certain of Oxygen's own future and goals: Oxygen should strive to be as successful as its parents, and most importantly, prepare the way for future offspring.

So in my mind Oxygen was something for the KDE 4.X series. Beyond that something new would have to take its place.

Its Present, where Past and Future face each-other

So you have this group of people, that are making an icon set, and in the constant struggle between past and future, you keep on creating new futures in order to move on, so you get more people involved in the project and you add new futures, new projects, new ideas, and the icon theme becomes so much more. This is the explosion phase. An icon theme becomes a Qt theme, a sound theme, a design platform – 1000 different things! Personally, this is the time that made me a designer. Never underestimate the power of trial and error. A lot of practice does not make perfect but it sure helps you to get better. The icon set suffered many mutations as it defined itself thought time, the Qt theme, Plasma themes, Oxygen and Air, the cursor theme, the sound theme, the multiple websites, the countless posters, banners, mugs, pins, meetings, talks, etc, etc,... amounted to gargantuan amounts of work. Make no mistake it was an absurd and gigantic effort, it was incredibly fun and in a way it set, what I personally consider, Oxygen biggest achievement. Before Oxygen, design projects in the open source world tended to vary from uncoordinated projects that lived in the same space, to vaguely related projects where different groups would coordinate design visions so that desktops would have some sort of coherent visual language, for example: the good efforts from our friends at the GNOME Desktop, and the multitude of projects it created but that shared an obvious vision and language. Still Oxygen was different now. It was so much more than just an icon theme. It was anything you would see in your desktop and more. We went to the extreme of making GTK themes so that the KDE experience would be even more consistent for the users. Hat tip to a great Oxygen guy, Hugo Pereira for his outstanding work in this area. Oxygen might not have been the best icon set of all times (it was good enough in my opinion but not as ground breaking as its parents were) but the scope of design efforts was unprecedented in the open source world. So to me, Oxygen's development period, "present", was a success - maybe not from the pure creativity design language point of view (I'm not even sure if

I'm unbiased to say anything truly fair about its merits in that regard), but from what it set as the goal post of what a design project in open source should be. I believe it did reach its goal by setting a new high bar in what to expect from open source design projects.

Its Future or the starting of a new Past

Some years ago Qt released Qt 5.0 and, as anyone that knows something about KDE knows, that means big changes are coming. Add to that the mobile explosion, the touch explosion, the QML language and Qt Quick revolutionizing things and the relative importance of design in computer user interfaces. This meant that visual languages and user expectations were changing. Also my expiration date on Oxygen was reaching its due date with series 5.X's on the horizon.

A perspective of making themes, even coordinated ones were not enough to create meaningful competitive user experiences. Oxygen failed to be that. As a result of the way it evolved and what it consisted of in its inception it was hard to be anything else than what it was. This new method of doing things in some ways would defeat the propose of consistent theming, just like architecture and urbanism rules are different things, so are consistent theming and perfectly tailored user experiences different and not fully compatible concepts. So at the end of the Oxygen period, user experience and user interface design was reaching an inflection point. Gone were the days were graphical designers challenged their own illustration skills in a perpetual "I can draw my candy more naturalisticly silly than yours". We had reached the saturation point of the silliness in graphic representations of every day objects as user interface elements. Now back then people needed to find a culprit for it all, a quintessential word that in itself represented all evil. Cue in "skeuomorphism", a word used in traditional design to imply a faux representation of a material. In this word we collectively found the "wrong" to be corrected. We had our culprit. Well all of this to me, back then, sounded a bit like a personal attack. I mean, gradients and shadows was all I did, and just because some were abusing it I had to pay for it? Yeap I did!

Plus Oxygen was starting to look old, in my eyes, and I knew it was time for something new, something fresh. The true testament to Oxygen's relevance was about to be put to a test. Would it be replaced, would some breeze of freshness be able to correct all wrongs in Oxygen? To be absolutely honest, I was worried. For some time it seemed no-one would pick up the work, and from a personal point of view I felt I needed to take some timeout to reinvent myself, so I should not be leading a post-Oxygen design language.

But the magic of open source did offer us, collectively, a new set of fresh people in the form of the KDE Visual Design Group, and with that Breeze, a new past of something new that was its future.

Oxygen will still live on the 5.X's series of Plasma/KDE desktops and I will keep on maintaining it, but now there is a new being that Oxygen failed to be. And it is great. This was achieved by far more than just me, it was/is a wonderful group of people - some of them I mention above, and trying to mention them all is impossible; but being incredibly unfair to all of the ones I will not mention, a word to Riccardo, Marco, Sho, Bettio, Ken, and all of the users: an enormous Thank You.

Conclusion

So when starting this article the point I wanted to make was the transient nature of design in open source projects. Its announced death at inception time is not something to be taken as a bad thing. It is a natural event that should be embraced from the beginning, the fact that it will have three tempos and that they will cross within themselves is a natural thing, on its way to reach conclusion, that its mortality is nothing but a step into a new birth. I wanted to say that I knew this from the beginning and that it made me happy that everything went as planned. It did and it is true that I am sincerely happy about the little apparent loop of creation, the cheating of death by continuity, a glimpse of immortality, via the ever chaotic butterfly effect. And this would make a nice enough conclusion advising you, the designers, to embrace open source projects with that in mind.

But... Thinking a bit more about it, I have to be more honest, I have to look into what drove me, what motivated me. I mean having a plan and executing it when you previously define that very plan according to a pattern that you see as the only possible best outcome may feel a bit mechanical, and it was nothing like that.

... and then I remember, people used to ask me all the time "how come you do it?" and I would answer "because it's fun", this simple answer was my real truth, maybe this is all it boils down to, that terrible cliché. It's not the destination it's the journey, the journey is what makes life and at the end of the day life is only true if you do, see, feel, create, quit, restart, win, lose, and love, yes love. Love what you do! I Loved doing Oxygen. I love doing open source design.

33 Say Yes

Jens Reuterberg

Jens Reuterberg is an illustrator and designer (but always illustrator first) living in Sweden with husband, cat and laptop. Since 2012 he has used Open Source for work exclusively, and since 2014 as his work exclusively since he started KDE's Visual Design Group. Sources have it he even talks in his sleep.

There are things in life that shape you. The little things that make your life take a sharp turn and wheer off in an entirely different direction. They happen constantly, it's how you met your partner, it's how you got the new job, it's how you got started playing the banjo. Often they are tiny little incidents of no remarkable relevance in and of themselves. A man slips on the concrete, you laugh and someone else laughs - you start to talk while in the background he brushes himself off and walk away and five nights later you wake up next to them and wonder how you could have even considered life "living" before.

We take them for granted, the little strange happenings that you can't foresee. Like they where a natural effect to you being you. How could you NOT have started playing the banjo, you might ask yourself. If it wasn't for that time you by mistake ordered one online you would probably have picked one up at some point, wouldn't you? It is amazing that, with the billions of us living here on a huge mass of land, the small chance that any one of us would meet any specific one of everyone else of us, is never really remarked upon with greater fascination than it currently is. Like it "just happened". Or how from an impossibly large selection of options you just chose the right one, at the right time, while being in the right frame of mind. It just happened.

In my opinion - the method with which to gain the greatest amount of "just happenings" is to allow for the little off-chance things to happen, to the greatest extent of its capacity. Let go. Say yes. Go "oh just this once" once more. Accept that you will look like an arse no matter what you do, so you might do it anyway and in a way you yourself could foresee and somewhat control than by just the act of being you every day.

That is why I am in KDE now. My willingness to look like a complete and utter arse. My readiness to say "yes" to things I am not totally sure about.

Obviously this is not the only reason. Other people's capacity to accept me even though I look like an arse are just as relevant as my own ability to be one, of course. Others' willingness to ask, is as important as my ability to say "yes". But that is, simplistically, the reason why I am in KDE at any rate. Saying "yes". Looking like an arse. But mostly saying "yes".

I was asked by Sebastian Kûgler to show up at the Plasma Sprint in Barcelona. He in turn had had me suggested to him by Aaron Seigo and those two, my "yes" and ability and acceptance of risking to look like arse was why I was standing outside of Barcelona airport alone.

Now I am a fairly awkward person. I know this. I can be either painfully silent and withdrawn or overly jovial and with the voice and body language of an opera singer for the hard of hearing having a stroke. Standing outside an airport, about to go to an office filled with strange programmers, a profession I don't grasp at all, about to do "design-stuff" for a week in an area I had never worked in before in my life, Open Source - I was in "silent-mode". At that point, grabbing a smoke between flight and bus ride, I regretted it greatly. I wanted nothing more than to go back home. To be fair I had spent the entire flight from Sweden regretting it. The bus ride from my home to the airport outside of Gothenburg had been a clear and constant battle to tell the bus driver to stop because I'd gotten on the wrong bus and had to walk back home through the woods. The act of going out the door was the emotional equivalence of a nuclear bomb strike of regret - regretting I had ever said "yes" when Sebastian asked me.

But it is those slapdash and shot-from-the-hip yeses that do it and that understanding was what had made me say it in the first place. Saying a skeptical "no" makes things easier but it's the yeses that deliver the potential for "just happens".

Not that I cared then for the bravery of my past. It's so easy to be brave before the battle. So simple to be self-confident before the test. To say "yes" then when you now want to scream "no".

I spent the bus ride from the airport into town in abject terror and was dumped at Plaça d'Espanya with suitcase, hand-drawn map and confusing self-doubt about the whole thing. What was I meant to do there? I had this vision of me, sitting alone in a corner checking Facebook and pretending to laugh at C++ jokes while work went on around me. Of questions with answers I could hardly spell - let alone deliver - and a group of programmers lying about having to all go to the loo in another area of town at the same time just so they could have beers and ask each other "why this Swedish mustaschioed dickhead is here". If optimism and hope for the future is a blue bird swooping through the sky, I was a bright orange elephant trying to maneuver a burning 747.

Now had I, at that time been able to see just a few days into the future - had I been able to, from that chance online encounter, question and temporarily insane "yes" on my part, extrapolate what would come, I would have been happy as nothing to be there. You see, KDE is a mess of people. Tons of us and all going in [Number of KDE people]+1 different directions at the same time. We stretch a rather broad gamut of humans, from the loud to the quiet, the kind to the apathetic, the professionals and the hobbyists, the productive to the lazy. "Anyone can join this club" could have been an insult, but for KDE it is more like a battle cry of clear intent. Had I known then, that the week that followed was not just productive and thought provoking but fun, I wouldn't have been nervous at all. Had I known I would meet people who I now consider close friends, who have that rather adorable quality of being incredibly intelligent, but seemingly not able to grasp how much more intelligent they actually are, treating some random Swedish arse as an equal instead as a befuddled moron - well I would be cartwheeling all the way through Barcelona to get to the sprint. In the days to come I talked technically complex issues with people who can do what is best summarized as "magic" as far as I'm concerned, people who didn't talk down to me, who didn't ignore me but instead explained every issue in a way that I could take part. Who listened to my ideas and more importantly explained why some of them would not work and some might. I talked about design with people who listened to me, asked questions and suggested ideas with the casual ease of a giraffe eating a trimmed hedge. People who inspired, not just amazing work in me but amazing work with them. Had I known, at that time, on that street, that I would go home later that week, fall asleep next to my husband and dream about interaction design, UX and visual elements and wake up the next morning pouring all energy into this "Open Source" thing - I would probably not have believed myself anyway, but if I had I wouldn't have been the least bit worried or scared of having said that initial "yes".

But I hadn't so I was, as I stumbled along that street through Barcelona with my map, backpack and social anxieties in tow.

I had drawn the front door of the Blue Systems office by hand on a piece of paper from Google Streetview simply because at the time that had felt more calming than taking a screenshot and the little drawing I kept holding up to compare different doors to was getting damp and soggy from my sweaty hands. When I found the door, that was also the moment I met my first KDE developer: Ivan.

I don't know what clued me off to him being one of the developers. It could have been the bags since he had also come from the airport or maybe it's the nerds innate ability to recognize a sibling but I asked "You here for the Plasma Sprint?" He looked at me as if he had yet to deduce if I was there to murder him, or just rob the office. As if some kind of debate on whether to pretend not to speak English and walk away or reply was raging inside him.

After a rather too long second or five he seemed to make up his mind, take his chances and go "yeeees...?", pressed the intercom to the front door, opened it and let me in.

34 Future Journeys: Which Path to Take?

Ben Cooksley

Ben Cooksley has been a user of free software since 2005, when he stumbled across a Knoppix CD. Since then he has gone on to wear many hats in the KDE project including user support, development, and more recently infrastructure administrator. When not working on KDE he can be found in places he previously hasn't visited or on nature trails.

As being a well established and successful community, KDE has accomplished a great deal by producing software for a wide variety of roles while having a good deal of fun along the way (although some hair may have been lost, depending on who you ask). We have produced countless different desktops and applications that users love, something proven by the wide variety of user customization and other content that exists for them. But we are not finished yet. The next evolution in technology, and along with it users' devices, awaits us.

Being ready for this evolution is crucial. Countless examples of titans not being ready for change exist: IBM underestimating Microsoft and Intel in the PC revolution; both Microsoft and Nokia failing to ride the smartphone revolution, all despite their former successes. With the rise of smartphones and their attached app stores, our traditional base of both users and new contributors is changing as well and will continue to do so as the next evolution arrives. We must change with it, bringing our software to new places and creating better software others haven't yet thought of.

If you think back to how you got involved in free software, chances are it started with you using the software in some form. Whether it was a bug that bit you, a feature you missed, documentation that lacked answers to your questions or something else, the road to involvement in free software communities such as KDE starts with becoming a user of the software it produces. It certainly did for me. Without a presence on these platforms, people cannot become even aware of our software, let alone try it and become a devoted user. With today's users being tomorrow's contributors, we cannot afford to miss new platforms as contributors are the lifeblood of not only our, but many other, free software communities.

The creation of better software sounds like a daunting task, like climbing a mountain with no prior experience of doing so. The truth is, the best software is the software that meets the needs of our particular use case the best and presents it in the most accessible form possible. This requires knowing the needs of the particular group of users, what issues they hit, the features they miss, and the things which get in their way. From there, we can set about solving these problems, climbing the mountain as it were, and creating a community of enthusiastic users for whom our software is best in class. In the long term, these very same users will not only spread our software but some will also become contributors, joining the communities that produced the software.

While the path forward may not be entirely known yet, the next 20 years hold many things in store for KDE. Our future software will run on devices we have yet to conceive of and will do things for our users that have yet to even be dreamed of. Yet one thing will remain the same – the creation of software people love – that will inspire the next group of contributors to our community.

35 Staying Relevant

Albert Vaca

Albert Vaca is a software developer from sunny Barcelona, with experience in Android and C++. He maintains the KDE Connect app for Android and PC.

When I was first asked to talk about KDE's history, I thought that I am much too new a member of the community to have something interesting to say. My first contact with KDE (as in "the KDE desktop") was in 2006, and I didn't touch any code until 2010. However, maybe with some luck, my experience as a relative newcomer might bring a different point of view to the whole picture.

The first thing I want to note is that I first approached Linux and the free software world in a time when it was booming. The market share of the Linux desktop was not huge, but free software was trendy: schools and public administrations were adopting it (even if only to save costs), it was in the news, a lot of innovation in browsers, in security and in other areas came from open source projects. For all of these reasons, it was a time when a lot of people, who like me were interested in geeky-computery-stuff, got into the free software world.

Many have said that one of the reasons for this boom was the failure of Windows Vista. And yes, Vista was not a success, but in hindsight it was probably the least of the problems Microsoft would have to face. The major game changer, in my opinion, came a bit later: the popularization of the smartphone. And there, the Linux desktop was hit in the same way Microsoft Windows was.

The reality is that, after the smartphone revolution, personal computers are not that relevant anymore. Therefore, in my opinion, the less relevant the desktop is, the less relevant we are as a community:

most people get into the KDE Community through our desktop environment and desktop apps.

This means, to start with, that we will not see that many geeky teenagers like me coming to us. This is perfectly normal: people today are more interested in context-aware, notification-enabled Android and iPhone apps, than in big bulky desktop suites that you manually launch to perform a task. Sadly, there is not much free software available on these new platforms.

Our current situation is that most people in KDE are people who work on and know about desktop software. Of course, most of these people are not going to stop developing for the desktop just because it is not trendy anymore. Instead, what I would like to see happen is engagement with a new generation of developers who have the ability to grow within KDE a new family of products relevant for them and the way they use the technology. That is, a generation of developers who understand what needs to be done in order to reach the users of the emerging platforms, and who want to do it from within free software.

Only by achieving this will we manage to reach a whole new generation of people and get them interested in using (and maybe eventually developing) free software, and to continue to grow our community. We are faced with non-free software, but in the same way we did it in the Windows monopoly era, I am sure we will put our focus again on providing software which fits the users' needs better. On these new platforms, there are plenty of new areas where free software can excel above non-free. Probably the most important one: the privacy of users.

At the same time, of course, we still need to maintain our position as one of the best desktop free software communities in the world. Here, though, we can learn a lot from the emerging platforms and adopt what they did well. Just to name a few things: sandboxed apps with discrete permissions, great focus on the user experience, standardized distribution mechanisms from developers to users, context-aware apps, and more. Non-free desktop platforms are also trying to do the same (an example of this are the dramatic

UI changes we have seen in each version of Windows from 7 to 10), so we have the opportunity to have a big impact by being, one more time, faster than them.

In conclusion, even though the personal computer is not going to die anytime soon, things are changing fast and we need to keep up with the good work we have been doing until now. At the same time, though, I think we need to find a way to reach all the people who don't use traditional desktop software, but who we believe would benefit from using free software.

We need to understand what we use technology for and how we can make sure that it serves our society now and in the future. We all agree that free software is the way to achieve this goal, so we have to make sure it is present on every front where technology is involved. It is then when we will be the platform that makes possible the society we believe in.

36 Software, Freedom and Beyond

Riccardo Iaconelli

Riccardo Iaconelli is a KDE developer since a very young age. He made his first steps in the open source world within FSFE and never stopped. He counts in his portfolio important collaborations with entities such as CERN or INFN. His latest project is WikiToLearn, a web platform dedicated to the creation and exploitation of free scientific knowledge.

I have been a KDE developer for more than half of my life now. KDE is turning 20 this year, making it one of the longest living (and most successful) open source communities in the world. I have performed almost any kind of tasks in all those years: I have been coding, translating, doing graphical work, promotion, even event organization or paperwork, when it was needed. I am so grateful to the community for the experiences I have made, that I am writing this essay with slightly wet eyes. KDE has been a central part of my education, one I could not do without. KDE is, today, about to face many new challenges. To be able to tackle them effectively, we need to know what made us strong, during all this time. I don't presume to have the answer, but I will share my story, in the hope that it will be useful.

So, how did I get interested in Free Software, in the first place? Well, I had the luxury of learning how to code at a very young age: I was 9 and I wanted to build my own website about skating. So I started to learn what I needed: HTML and JavaScript. And then, of course, some PHP. But I got so intrigued by the programming world that I decided I was going to be a hacker, when I grew up. After much googling, I figured that the only way I could be a hacker, though, was to install Linux. I downloaded my first Linux distribution, a SuSE, and I installed it like I would with any other Windows application: I just kept pressing "Next" without caring to read what was going on. A minute later, I was there, without a bit of all of my data, applications and music, with an operating system I did not know, with no internet connection, but a strong will to "become a hacker" and learn. I installed and used just about every application I had on the SuSE DVD (I even went as far as installing and using an application to print out barcodes for hours). But it was not just technical work. I educated myself about the four freedoms of the GPL and why they mattered. And I found the community I wanted to be a part of: KDE.

I was, however, too shy to contribute to KDE through coding, even if I already knew some C++, so I started with the simplest job I could take on: translating. And I had lots of fun! So I continued, I became a core developer of Plasma, writing the first plasmoids, a core developer and a designer of Oxygen (working on the theme, window decoration, cursor theme, icons, wallpapers...) and many more things (from kdelibs to games to PIM). Probably the single piece of work (outside these big projects) I am most proud of is the complete redesign (and implementation) of Amarok's user interface in QML. It was sexy, but unfortunately it was never released. By getting my hands dirty I learned a lot from everyone in the community, trying to build new skills and expertise, to be used later. It was simply amazing.

There was not a single role model, but I had the luck of finding many great mentors within the community. In general, I tried to simply be attentive to other people, trying to find out what I like in what they do, and what I can learn from them. Once I see it, I start to apply those elements in my life, whether it's a personal lifestyle choice, a technical decision or a way to relate to others. This "growing together" is, in my opinion, the true spirit of free software.

It is partly due to this belief that I launched WikiToLearn, a KDE project which works with the greatest research centers, universities and experts, to share under free licenses the great amount of knowledge produced there, at Akademy in 2015 in La Coruña. We want to create free and collaborative textbooks, accessible to the world and always remixable, to teach the values of openness and collaboration to the next generation. I think that teaching why openness is important is crucial, if we want to keep the open movement as strong as it is now.

To motivate myself I always remind myself why I am doing what I am doing. I believe in a free world; I believe in the power of decentralization. I believe that the sum of our collective minds and efforts is greater than what any of us alone can achieve. And I want to have fun while doing what I am doing.

I feel that one of the challenges we are facing right now is evolution. How do we grow past a world which was entirely desktop-centric, and which now gives the desktop an important but no longer essential role? I think the answer lies in the community. We have to go back to our origins, to the universities where many of us started contributing. We have to see what is now interesting, explain the fun we can have developing in the open world and the importance of keeping a thriving open ecosystem.

We need to explain our strengths and bring them our experience. Here is what I usually suggest people to do: learn by doing, and always get great mentors to review your work. Get your hands dirty and teach yourself to code. Try, fail, try harder and iterate. And don't stop until you become perfect. Aim for elegance. Learn everything you can from the world and your peers, and never stop doing that. The challenge is with yourself, not with anyone else. How much better can you be?

This way, many years later, I found I have been growing with the community, learning many skills along the way. I watched subprojects flourishing and dying, and in this process shaping the meaning and essence of KDE. In all this period serving as core developer I have seen KDE grow and evolve beyond what we thought was our first goal, to face new and unimagined challenges, and expand towards directions we didn't even believe possible.

I have been a KDE developer for half of my life. KDE turns 20 this year, and I am 25. I want to continue to see this amazing community to flourish, and I want to play my part in the first project that I maintain, by adding yet another global success to our portfolio. And I think that with WikiToLearn we have all the right cards in our hands to achieve that. The KDE Community has been almost a family to me, and I just want to thank every member of it for making all this a reality.

37 A New Generation

Andreas Cord-Landwehr

Andreas Cord-Landwehr joined KDE in 2011 and primarily contributes to KDE's educational software applications. After his PhD at Paderborn University in the field of algorithmic game theory in spring 2016, he joined CLAAS E-Systems as a software developer.

When my aunt tells me about her youth, about using horses and carriages to harvest the hay at my grandparent's farm, it sounds like a story of long ago. When I tell some high school student about twenty years ago, about going to the library to borrow programming books, since we did not have access to the internet at home at that time, it must sound like a story as similarly ancient as my aunt's one. As hard as it is for me to imagine a world where we still use horses for our daily work, it might be similarly hard for someone of the "digital native" generation to understand the life in the world just twenty years ago – albeit it is just one generation.

Twenty years ago was the time of the struggle out of the Microsoft vendor lock-in. At that time everyone I knew used a Windows PC, even me. Actually, my KDE and Linux memories only start some years later. It must have been about fifteen years ago, when I got my first Linux Boot CD and got excited by a boot screen that really showed me what happens on the system instead of a Windows screen that liked to magically freeze during boot. Still, I can remember my first log-in into the KDE desktop, my first bug report, my first system configurations. It has been an exciting time. Updating the KDE desktop always brought tons of new features, new applications that I was missing from the Windows world, and I really felt the freedom and adventures this new world gave me. For me, as someone who joined the ranks of the KDE developers several years later, I can only guess how exciting the times must have been in particularly as a developer back then.

Today, the world is a different one. Linux is an important ecosystem and deeply rooted in the economy. The KDE desktop together with the Linux ecosystem provides applications for all needs and it is a rare event when one encounters a missing application from the Windows world; actually, sometimes at work I have it the other way around. However, the trend of the desktop as the predominant computing system is changing. In the economy, the desktop will surely remain and will still be an important tool for many decades to come. But for our daily lives it is already different. The desktop computer is slowly becoming an office tool, like a typewriter in old times, a thing that you do not place in your living room but rather in an office. Already today, the desktop computer is not the first device in your hand if you want to look up some information. Some years ago it was very different.

The question is, what does this mean for us as the KDE Community, a community that started around the goal of making a great desktop for end users. I believe that this new trend is both a challenge and an opportunity at once. We have our main products, which target the desktop, a solid platform which will still be used for a long time. But there are the new fields, the smart phones, the tablets, the watches, and the countless devices that try to make your life easier. Compared to our starting grounds the signs for these new fields are not bad. Actually free software found its way into many parts of these devices. Now we have to identify what the challenges are that we want to address in the future. With the KDE Vision in place we are in a good position for doing this.

One major challenger will be to find a good balance of what to preserve and what to start anew. We have a long tradition as an open source project but should not become a dinosaur waiting for a comet. We are active in hot topics, but should not become a flock of lemmings running mindlessly in one direction. In a community we are people of various backgrounds, educations and ages, and with twenty years completed, we finished what one can call a generation.

I wonder, how does someone perceive this world who is young enough that they cannot even remember KDE 4.0, a world that always had the internet, where the first access to a computer was swiping a hand. With each generation the perception of the world and of the way we deal with it is changing. This even changes the fights we see as worth fighting. As drastic as the change from horses to harvesters was, I see the change from the open source world twenty years ago, with the KDE desktop still being an infant, to today. But since not only the tools and techniques are changing, we as a community must evolve to the next level, to update the purpose that drives us. Twenty years are one human generation, I am curious what will be after another one.

Closing Words

When I joined the KDE Community 10 years ago I could never have imagined how much of an impact it would have on my life. I am where I am today because of the people in KDE and everything I learned from them. I am surely not the only one and I am grateful for it. In a world of rising tension between cultures, countries and people, communities like KDE transcend artificial barriers and make us understand that we are better together than we are apart, that we achieve more when we are united than when we are divided, that our shared interests are bigger than our differences.

This book can only give you a glimpse into the past 20 years of KDE. I hope we still gave you a good overview and explained why our heart is in this community.

To my fellow contributors: May you always stay innovative, smart, open-minded, inclusive, dedicated and awesome. Thank you for being a part of the journey. A lot of amazing things are still ahead of us.

To our users: The past 20 years have shown that there is a lot of technical excellence, pragmatism and will to fight for our users in this community. We will continue on this way - for you.

— Lydia Pintscher, President of KDE e.V.

Berlin, Germany; 24th of July 2016

www.ingramcontent.com/pod-product-compliance
Lightning Source LLC
Chambersburg PA
CBHW060847170526
45158CB00001B/262